Muffin Magic
... and More

Baking Secrets
Your Mother Never Told You

Kathleen Mayes

Woodbridge Press
Santa Barbara, California 93160

Also by Kathleen Mayes:

Another cookbook:

Boutique Bean Pot
(with co-author Sandra Gottfried)

Guides to good health and nutrition:

Beat Jet Lag
The Complete Guide to Digestive Health
Fighting Fat!
Osteoporosis: Brittle Bones and the Calcium Crisis
The Sodium-Watcher's Guide

Muffin Magic ... and More

Note to the reader

The information in this book is for general information and no responsibility is assumed on the part of the author or publisher for its application or use in any specific case or by any particular person.

It is not the purpose of this publication to guarantee any nutritional or medicinal preparation or the effectiveness thereof. This information is not presented with the intention of diagnosing or prescribing.

Any use of brand names in this book is for identification only, and does not imply endorsement or otherwise by the author or publisher.

Published and distributed by

Woodbridge Press Publishing Company
Post Office Box 6189
Santa Barbara, California 93160

Copyright © 1993 by Kathleen Mayes

Distributed simultaneously in the United States and Canada.
Printed in the United States of America.

Library of Congress Cataloging-in-Publication Data:

Mayes, Kathleen.
   Muffin magic ... and more : baking secrets your mother never told you / [Kathleen Mayes].
     p.   cm.
   Includes bibliographical references and index.
   ISBN 0-88007-201-6 : $12.95
   1. Muffins. I. Title.
TX770.M83M39 1993
641.8' 15—dc20   93-25105
                                               CIP

Front cover painting and text illustrations are by Janice Blair.

Contents

'Butters' without Fat   *Cranberry Spice De-Lites*
A User's Guide to Ginger   *Ginger Lite–Bread*
Lemons: Zest for Life   *Lemon Lite–Muffins*
New Wrinkles on Prunes   *Prune Pecan Lite–Bread*
Pumpkin Spread   *Pumpkin Bran Lites*
Cottage Cheese: A New Look
   at an Old Favorite   *Walnut Spice Wunderbars*

Appendix

Acknowledgments by the Author

I would like to thank family and friends (including my editor, Howard Weeks at Woodbridge Press) for valiantly tasting numerous baked samples. Their candid observations were of great value in developing the more innovative recipes.

I also want to express my warm appreciation for the generous cooperation given by the following companies and organizations:

American Institute of Baking, Manhattan, KS; American Mushroom Institute, Kennett Square, PA; Buderim Australian Ginger, San Ramon, CA; California Apricot Advisory Board, Walnut Creek, CA; California Prune Board (Food Technology), Pleasanton, CA; California Raisin Advisory Board, Fresno, CA; Castle & Cooke, Inc., San Francisco, CA; Church & Dwight Co., Inc., Princeton, NJ; Colorado State University Cooperative Extension, Fort Collins, CO; Dairy Council of Wisconsin, Westmont, IL; Edwards Mansion, Redlands, CA; Rebecca J. Eldridge, Santa Barbara Botanic Garden, Santa Barbara, CA; Ferrara Pan Candy Co., Forest Park, IL; First Colony Coffee & Tea Company, Norfolk, VA; Frieda's Finest/Produce Specialties, Inc., Los Angeles, CA; General Mills, Inc., Minneapolis, MN; Giurlani, USA, Fresno, CA; Jerseymaid Dairies, Los Angeles, CA; Ketchum Public Relations, San Francisco, CA (representing California prunes); Mott's, Menallen Township, Aspers, PA; Pet, Inc., St. Louis, MO; Pillsbury Company, Minneapolis, MN; Planters LifeSavers Company, Winston-Salem, NC; Richardson's Seaside Banana Garden, La Conchita, CA; Scott W. Sanders, Ph.D., Creative Food Consultants, Byron, CA; Shore, Young & Tomi, Inc., San Francisco, CA (representing California apricots); Sokol & Co., Countryside, IL; Specialty Brands, San Francisco, CA; Stonehill Farm Foods Corp., Schwenksville, PA; Sun-Diamond Growers of California, Stockton, CA; Williams-Sonoma, San Francisco, CA; Wisconsin Milk Marketing Board, Madison, WI.

And finally my special thanks to the helpful staff of the Goleta and Santa Barbara Public Libraries for responding so patiently to many requests for reference information.

Introduction

The perfect muffin

Can I tell you a secret? I've had this life-long quest for perfection—in a muffin, that is: to strive for and achieve the creation of a model muffin, beautifully domed, with tempting shades of richest brown on its outer crust, the most delicate and moist inside crumb, wholesome in flavor, whether perfumed just-so with the finest spices, the freshest herbs, or perhaps bejeweled with luscious fruit. What could be lovelier?

A small morsel perhaps, but one that's perfect for the occasion—dinner company arriving at short notice when you impulsively invite friends over; an accompaniment to a handsome vegetarian feast; a cozy family supper; a quick snack when long working hours demand something good to give you staying power or "comfort food"; a thoughtful gift for someone far from home, at school, at camp, in the military, or recuperating in the hospital.

Muffins can be *magical*—kitchen alchemy—doing much more than just rounding out a meal or filling up a plate. They're the most trendy of basic, comfort foods, back in style in the finest restaurants as well as our own kitchens, whether hearty or elegantly light, sweet or savory, reflecting a certain amount of nostalgia for food and entertaining ideas of the past, without silly pretensions. Imagine transforming a meal and elevating it to a special status—making a simple meal special or a superb meal sensational. Some muffins are perfect partners with foods, others proudly stand as masterpieces on their own, simply with a pot of hot fresh coffee or special aromatic tea for a companion. When do you eat them? Round the clock and round the calendar! They are an *any*-time-of-the-day food: a good day's start when you have no time for breakfast except a heated muffin from the microwave; happy mates for a quick salad or soup at lunch; or two-bite delicacies to serve with panache at a stylish buffet dinner.

11

A muffin can be sophisticated, made elegant with the addition of the finest ingredients to delight the epicure; or a simple assembly of a few foods remaining in the refrigerator at the end of the week, or the bountiful seasonal harvest from garden or farmer's market: apples or apricots, almonds or avocados, blueberries or blackberries, peaches or pumpkin. The ingredients of a muffin—sweet or savory—are only limited by your imagination. Almost everything works. They are enormously versatile to give an endless variety of types, textures and flavors with always-fresh appeal.

The magic of home-baking

Although America's tastes had turned the four basic food groups into "Take-in," "Eat-out," "Frozen" and "Canned," the trend of the future is toward retro-food—back to old-fashioned, homestyle dishes. We have come to realize that food is more than just eating and cooking: we're more concerned now about what we eat and how it affects us—and we still want food to taste great. It's a key player in our lives and our memories, and memory affects taste. Food cooked at home, shared at the table, is the most important aspect of living together; and sharing meals means sharing our lives and showing we care.

Why is home-baking superior? Many people are worried nowadays about the freshness and wholesomeness of foods in stores. Although muffins had gained a reputation for being healthful, the truth is that supermarket baked goods are over-priced, over-sized, overloaded with fat, cholesterol, sodium and calories, or heaven-knows-what chemicals, conditioners and preservatives. (Remember: smaller doesn't always mean better; more than half the calories in many commercial mini-muffins come from fat.) And with bakery muffins you don't even know what you're buying since they don't come with printed nutritional information. With the desire to return to a simpler life-style less dependent on commercial products, home-baking is a logical step in that direction. Simple. Natural. When you make muffins and quick-breads at home, you regain control of what you eat and prepare food with natural ingredients—not from a box (with its contents determined by big business)—but full of wholesome goodness and old-time nostalgia, and free of artificial preservatives and unnatural flavorings. Home bakers can easily increase the fiber in their diet, cut fat, sugar and sodium, and incorporate whole foods including whole grains into the muffins and quick-breads. When you make muffins with *nutritious* ingredients, they cease to be wicked indulgences of too many calories, saturated fats and sugar. Instead they become health-wise components of a wholesome diet rich in grains, fresh fruits and vegetables. The bonus is that they are super delicious!

Not only that, a return to the kitchen is a way to create, invent, do your own thing, and relieve stress in a busy world. Producing "somethin' lovin' from the oven" is a means of expressing love to family and true hospitality toward friends, showing a concern for their well-being and making good times special.

The magic begins when tantalizing *magnetic* aromas waft from the oven, and no one needs a second bidding to come to the dining table. Many people miss out on this delightful experience because they have never attempted what is really a simple task—making muffins and quick-breads from scratch. Some people feel they are too busy and that muffins are time-consuming. But there's nothing complicated or mysterious about them. They are almost effortless and can be put together by practically everyone—whether novice or expert; the kitchen equipment is modest and the time taken is minimal. No tricky yeast to fuss over, no kneading, no rising time, and start to finish can take less than an hour. But the results can be impressive. This divine food doesn't cost a fortune but gives pleasure beyond price. When you know the true worth of home-baking, you'll want to continue. Forever.

By the way, enjoying muffins doesn't have to give you a guilt complex if you're trying to lose a few pounds, because the "Ultralites" in Chapter 6 feature lowfat baking, showing the modern way to have your cake and diet too!

Breads and leavenings

For some background, let's have a look at the start of breads and muffins. As early as 17,000 years ago, ancient peoples along the Nile Valley were pounding wild grains on rocks, mixing in a little water, and pressing the mixture into rudimentary coarse-textured flat bread to be "baked" by drying in the sun. Five thousand years ago, Egyptians were growing wheat and barley, grinding the grain, pouring the batter into narrow molds and baking it in primitive beehive-shaped ovens. These early cooks then discovered that the bread was enhanced with a leavening, using the wild and natural mold strains that preceded commercial yeast, or by tearing off a piece of dough and using it to start the next day's batch—the original "sourdough."

At about the same time as the Egyptians, the Chinese also hit on the idea of making a light bread from fermented dough. Over the centuries, the milling of grains improved and yeasts were developed. Pliny the Elder reported that the ancient Gauls and Iberians had found skimmed beer-foam was good to leaven bread dough and this, he said, was why they had "a lighter kind of bread than other peoples." The French today remain the world's masters in the art of superb yeast-bread making.

Humans have often attached a deep mystical quality to bread, and many cultures believed the origin of wheat to be supernatural and a gift from heaven. Bread was a symbol of life, and was considered sacred: loaves were placed in royal Egyptian tombs for the journey of the deceased after death. Early Saxons in Britain offered specially baked loaves to God from the first harvest of the season; Swedes molded dough shaped into female figures in gratitude for the earth's fertility.

Muffins in the Old World

The word "muffin" appears to have originated in the Middle Ages, probably from the Lower German language, where *muffen* was the plural of *muffe* meaning "cake." "Muffin" may also be connected with the Old French word *moufflet* meaning "soft."

At any rate, muffins became part of the language in Britain and by the eighteenth century a daily commodity in bakers' shops. In 1766, Christopher Anstey in his *Bath Guide* to the elegant meeting rooms of that spa city, commented:

I freely will own I the Muffins preferr'd
To all the genteel Conversation I heard.

The muffin man was commonly seen on the streets of London and other cities in Britain until as recently as sixty years ago, along with young girls selling fragrant lavender from Norwich or sweet red cherries from Kentish orchards, the swarthy men from France and Spain hawking strings of large yellow onions, the scissor-grinder, and the "rag-and-bone" men trading on household discards. All had their distinctive cries. In winter months, the muffin man would walk the streets, carrying a cloth-covered basket filled with muffins from local bakeries, ringing his handbell to attract housewives or their maidservants:

Muffins and crumpets and pies and Yule do's.
Pay me a ha'penny and take what you choose!

In 1851, Henry Mayhew in *London Labour and the London Poor* quoted a fourteen-year-old muffin "man" on his trade:

"I turns out muffins and crumpets, sir, in October, and continues until it gets well into spring, according to the weather. I carries a first-rate article; werry much so. If you was to taste 'em, sir, you'd say the same. If I sell three dozen muffins at ha'penny each, and twice that in crumpets, it's a werry fair day, werry fair. ... If there's any unsold, a coffee-shop gets them cheap, and puts 'em off cheap again next morning.

"I didn't hear of any street-seller who made the muffins or crumpets he vended. Indeed, he couldn't make the small quantity required so as to be remunerative. The muffins are bought off the bakers, and at prices to leave a profit of fourpence in a shilling. ... The muffin man carries his delicacies in a basket, well swathed in flannel, to retain the heat. People like them warm, sir, to satisfy them they're fresh, and they almost always are fresh; but it can't matter so much about their being warm, as they have to be toasted again. I only wish butter was a sight cheaper, and that would make the muffins go. ...

"My best customers is genteel houses, 'cause I sells a genteel thing. I likes wet days best, 'cause there's werry respectable ladies what don't keep a servant, and they buys to save themselves going out. We're a great convenience to the ladies, sir—a great convenience to them as likes a slap-up tea."

At the other end of the social spectrum, the serving of hot muffins in Victorian gentlemen's clubs was conducted with such pomp as to be almost a religious ceremony. According to Sir Clough Williams-Ellis of London:

"Muffins would come in their heated covered silver dish along with salt cellar, China tea, cream and folded napkin, and be set down at my elbow by a club waiter still in the livery of the Regency—knee-breeches, silk stockings and buckled shoes—and all for no more than a shilling."

In Victorian homes where muffins or crumpets were an important part of the winter tea-time ritual, drawing-rooms would have a "muffin stand" (a small three-tiered table) for holding toasted muffins, sandwiches, cakes and the teacups. Well-laid tea-tables would bear a silver, glass or china caster called a "muffineer" used for sprinkling hot muffins with cinnamon or other spices. And a "muffin-worry" was a colloquial term in those days for an old ladies' tea party. Although in the 1840s, the clang of the muffin man's bell was prohibited by Act of Parliament, the ban was ignored and didn't remain operative because this tradesman was popular among the people.

The muffin man is no longer seen in city streets today, and muffins are considered essentially old-fashioned fare (although it is said that a sole surviving muffin man still supplies the occupants of Buckingham Palace). Only his memory lives on in the nursery rhyme:

O do you know the Muffin Man?
O do you know his name?
O do you know the Muffin Man
Who lives in Drury Lane?

Well, what are or were the muffins and crumpets that the bell-ringing muffin man used to sell for a halfpenny each? Up to this time, the leavening used for bread-making had been yeasts and the air incorporated into the dough during kneading, so these English specialties were yeast risen, had a soft dough and not a poured batter, and were baked in metal rings. The inside crumb had distinctive large holes—the *English* muffin.

Muffins in the New World

In the meantime, American bakers were beginning to diverge from the practices of their English counterparts by experimenting with substitutes for yeast in bread-making.

The basic idea about leavening in baking is to create carbon dioxide gas, whether generated from yeast, sourdough or baking powder. In the United States, the first use of a crude baking powder occurred in the 1790s. Cooks had been trying to make non-yeast breads by using *pearl-ash* (potassium carbonate) made from the ashes that remained after burning wood or corncobs, but it was an arduous task for the breadmaker. The pearl-ash, when moistened and heated, did produce carbon dioxide that caused the bread to rise slightly, but as cooks tried increasing the amounts they added to dough, the ingredient's bitter flavor spurred the search for alternatives that were more palatable.

Another leavening originating in Germany was powdered horn, made from the antlers of harts and deer. The modern equivalent of hartshorn (ammonium carbonate, available in drug stores) is still used for cookie baking in Germany and Scandinavia.

Perhaps the fast increase in the development and use of baking powders for leavening in the United States was due to the American love of speed and the element of novelty. At the same time, people were on the move migrating West, looking for short cuts: little or no time could be wasted on waiting for yeast dough to rise at the end of a long tiring day on the trail or on the farm, when hungry families wanted bread on the table. The new-fangled quick-breads fitted into the picture because they didn't have to be kneaded or allowed time to rise before baking.

The story goes that when covered wagons passed the Great Salt Lake in Utah, the pioneers along the route discovered large natural deposits of *saleratus*, better known now as baking soda (or sodium bicarbonate). The women gathered up handfuls of the mineral from the ground, mixed a little in their dough with buttermilk, soured milk or cream, and after finding it had good rising power, they would write home enthusiastically "it makes splendid bread." Large deposits of soda were later discovered at an old evaporated lake in Wyoming, and this source is still utilized today.

There was also a religion-inspired effort during the nineteenth century by zealots connected with the Temperance Movement, to steer Americans away from yeast (because yeast, even in bread, produces alcohol), and to use other leavening alternatives.

Still, doctors across the country were concerned that health was endangered by the habit of bolting biscuits "ominously yellow with imperfectly neutralized saleratus." It was a chancy business for cooks to achieve the right balance with crude saleratus, since the effective strength was variable and results were never twice the same. Some must have caused horrible indigestion.

Around 1835 the first tartrate baking powder was developed as a substitute for yeast in breads and cakes, produced from a combination of sodium bicarbonate and tartaric acid (cream of tartar, the residue scraped from wine barrels). The tartaric acid was to give the mixture a souring potential, to get around the necessity of adding one (such as sour milk) to the batter. In 1850, the company of Preston & Merrill of Boston, Massachusetts, was the first to manufacture a baking powder with such a formula and market it on a commercial scale.

In another venture, an analytical chemist Professor Eben Norton Horsford, developed a baking powder in the 1850s that was so successful it enabled him to retire at a young age. In the 1860s and 1870s the agents for "Horsford's Self-Raising Bread Preparation" popularized his new baking powder by claiming it prevented rickets, cholera and tooth decay, and even promoted muscle and bone growth! Unlike yeast, they advertised, it did *not* produce alcohol—it made gas.

During the same period, muffins in some parts of the country came to be known as cornmeal "gems," the word *Gem* coming from the name of a commercial baking powder used as leavening. However they were not always gemlike, and the home baker was often taking a gamble: baking powders varied in reliability, questionable bleaches were being used to hasten the whitening of flours, and adulteration of foods was rampant.

Cookbook authors were so uncertain and suspicious of product purity, they cautiously continued to instruct readers to use only proportions of plain baking soda and cream of tartar. Go through your grandmother's collection of cookbooks of 100 or 150 years ago, and you'll rarely find mention of ready-prepared baking powder. For instance, in 1879, Marion Cabell Tyree in her *Housekeeping in Old Virginia* was still giving recipes for muffins leavened with soda and cream of tartar and baked in novelty "snow-ball cups." Other cookbook authors nervously specified both yeast as well as baking powder in the same recipe, to avoid failure.

(Baking in those days had other hazards too, such as the unscientific way of judging oven temperature, long before modern thermostat control: the customary method to evaluate the heat of an oven was to thrust a hand in and count seconds until the cook was forced to pull it out with a faint scream—twenty-four seconds meant moderate; twelve seconds was *hot*.)

However, by the end of the nineteenth century, manufacturers became more confident about purity and quality, and were advertising baking powders that would guarantee the creation of the desired spongy texture in baked goods.

It's a relief to know that after the trials and tribulations of the past, the home-cook of today is assured of baking muffins of superb quality using a range of consistent ingredients, and can rely on the highest possible standards of purity.

Chapter 1

What Goes in a Muffin?

The fun thing to remember is that almost anything goes! Muffins are versatile so you can show inventiveness and throw in almost any healthy ingredients—in the right proportions—and achieve success. The recipes in this book are only the starting point from which to launch your own cooking ideas and create imaginative variations. Baking, after all, is an individual art, and no one will come after you if you go against the grain. For best results, ingredients should be as fresh as possible and of the finest quality your budget can manage.

Flours

Although flour would seem to be a basically simple ingredient, there's more to it than meets the eye, and it pays to know more about it: what baking qualities it has, and how the different flours vary.

All recipes here use flour that has been milled from wheat, because it gives consistently good results. Most importantly, wheat grain contains proteins that form *gluten* when mixed with liquids, and the elastic texture of the gluten holds the bubbles produced by leavening, but you can experiment with other flours and grains, to see which ones produce the results you're looking for. Check the shelves of your health-food store and whole-food store for the different types; Appendix 3 gives a list of mills that can supply specialty flours as well as whole grains, seeds and spices.

Flour labeled *all-purpose* is generally a blend of hard and soft wheat: *hard*-wheat flours are usually from spring wheat from the West, Midwest and Southwest, and noted for their mineral content and for making firm, rather elastic breads; *soft*-wheat flours are often from the Midwest, and contribute a smoothness. Flour may yield different results in different parts of the country, because major national flour mills use different blending formulas to suit regional preferences. They speculate that a Northerner tends to bake more bread, and the Southerner more biscuits, hence the Northern formula has a higher proportion of hard wheat, and the Southern formula more soft wheat.

All-purpose flour is finely milled from just the endosperm, the inner part of the wheat kernel, so the bran (outer section of the kernel) and wheat germ (sprouting section) have been removed (see figure). Then the millers return to the flour the nutrients iron, thiamine, riboflavin and niacin that had been in the bran and germ of the kernel. The flour is bleached with chlorine dioxide and treated with a maturing agent (potassium bromate or iodate) that oxidizes and ages the flour to strengthen the gluten content.

Unbleached all-purpose flour is superior because, although it too is milled from only the endosperm of the kernel, with germ and bran removed, it hasn't been treated with artificial bleach. Being unbleached doesn't affect baking results but it does produce a more natural flavor.

Whole-wheat flour is milled from the entire kernel of the wheat, including the bran, the germ and all, making it rich in protein, minerals and other nutritional goodies, and giving it a pleasant nutty flavor. Because this flour contains the wheat germ, it has a higher fat content and is apt to deteriorate more quickly; it's best to buy whole-wheat flour in small quantities, store it in an air-tight container in the refrigerator or freezer, and bring it to room temperature just before using. Whole-wheat pastry flour is more suited to making muffins, pancakes, cookies and pastries. If the sack doesn't specify either "pastry flour" or "bread flour," it's probably all-purpose, milled and blended from both hard and soft varieties of wheat.

Other flours include:

Bread flour—whole-wheat or white—milled and blended primarily for yeast baking, has high-gluten content, and is not used in these recipes.

Buckwheat flour. This flour is usually sold in health-food stores and specialty-food markets. Buckwheat is often confused with wheat, but it's a member of another plant family, and the flour gives a hearty, full-bodied flavor. Because of its reduced gluten capacity, use only about 1 cup buckwheat flour as a substitute for an equal amount of all-purpose flour in any dozen-muffin recipe.

Cornmeal. You can use either yellow or white. Because corn kernels contain no gluten, muffins made entirely of cornmeal don't work, but for that distinctive gritty crunchiness you can substitute up to 1 cup of cornmeal for an equal amount of all-purpose flour in a dozen-muffin recipe. Italian-type cornmeal called *polenta,* coarsely ground from corn kernels, makes particularly good corn muffins and corn sticks.

Gluten flour, which is basically a wheat flour with the starch removed, is sometimes recommended for people on special diets. It's a good addition to quick-breads when working with low-gluten grains as rye, corn, oats, barley, soy or triticale.

Graham flour, developed by the Reverend Dr. Sylvester Graham (a 19th century Connecticut doctor and preacher of good health through nutrition), is a coarsely ground whole-wheat flour. Making muffins entirely with whole-wheat or Graham flour is not usually a good idea since they make the dough heavy and dense. You generally get better results by combining equal amounts of all-purpose flour and whole-wheat flour in recipes. That way, gluten structure is improved for a finer texture and better rising power.

Oat flour, which doesn't have the same gluten-forming ability of wheat flour, produces muffins that are lower in volume but more moist. Use only in small quantities (about ½ cup) with all-purpose flour in any dozen-muffin recipe.

Rye flour. If you substitute rye flour for all-purpose flour, results may be disappointing since it also is low in gluten and the muffins will be low-rising, more compact, and have a somewhat unattractive grey tinge. Store rye flour in the refrigerator or freezer in an airtight container. Use no more than ½ cup in any dozen-muffin recipe.

Self-rising flour which usually consists of less hard wheat and more soft wheat, is mostly sold in the Southern states. The blend usually contains 1½ teaspoons baking powder and ½ teaspoon salt per cup of flour. If you are using this type of flour instead of all-purpose flour, you'll need to omit the recipe's salt and baking powder.

Soybean flour, available in health-food stores and whole-food stores, has a higher protein content and may be added in small amounts to enrich all-purpose wheat flour.

When buying any type of flour, be sure that market supplies are fresh and have been properly stored, to retain the right moisture balance, and then remember to treat it properly when you bring it home: transfer flour from the paper sack into a large glass jar or tightly lidded container and you'll help protect it from humidity changes and bug invasions. If left in its original bag, flour will readily absorb or lose moisture, depending on the weather, where you live and storage conditions. During the warm humid days of summer or moist regions of the country, flour often has an increased moistness; during winter or in the desert, it tends to have less. Dried-out flour will make a stiff batter—and that makes a terribly dry muffin.

Leavening agents

Breads, quick-breads and muffins would be heavy, flat and indigestible lumps without leavening. Chemical leavening works by developing carbon dioxide gas to lighten the flour mixture, hence all recipes here call for baking powder and/or baking soda.

Baking powder is a fine blend of bicarbonate of soda with an acidic material such as tartaric acid and a base of starch or flour. In most recipes, you sift baking powder with the flour to distribute it evenly and to give a uniform texture before adding the liquid ingredients. Have you ever wondered what "double-acting" means on that tin of baking powder? "Double-acting" indicates that carbon dioxide will be triggered in two stages—a small amount is first given off when the powder is moistened during mixing, then the gas expands a second time when heat is applied. This feature makes it useful when the baking is to be done a considerable time after mixing.

Store baking powder in a dry place and be sure it's fresh. If you're in doubt about its age, test a teaspoon of powder in ½ cup hot water. It should fizz strongly, otherwise throw it out and buy a new box.

Generally, the ratio in a recipe is 1 teaspoon baking powder to 1 cup of flour, but if you're including whole-wheat flour or a lot of fruit or nuts, use 1½ teaspoons per cup of flour. If several well-beaten eggs are in the recipe, you usually reduce the amount of baking powder.

Baking powders usually contain aluminum sulfate which some people don't care to use. If you can't find a commercial baking powder without aluminum sulfate (try health-food stores first), make your own compound as a substitute for each teaspoon baking powder. Combine:

½ teaspoon cream of tartar (potassium bitartrate)
¼ teaspoon baking soda
¼ teaspoon cornstarch

The cornstarch absorbs moisture in the air and prevents premature chemical reaction. Work fast when using home-made baking powder because the carbon dioxide gas is released more quickly and at a lower temperature than is the case with commercial double-acting powders.

Baking soda, or bicarbonate of soda, is another leavening agent and one that needs something acidic, such as sour milk, fruit, fruit juices or molasses in the recipe, in order to trigger the release of carbon dioxide which makes the batter rise. You generally add about ½ teaspoon soda for each cup of sour milk, sour cream, buttermilk, yogurt or juice. You'll notice the "Ultralite" recipes in Chapter 6 have a small increase in soda to balance the fruit purées.

Eggs

Not only do they give a wonderful richness to quick-breads and muffins, they add nutrients, improve the flavor and deepen the color. When eggs are well-beaten, they enclose air in tiny cells which help to lighten the batter mixture. Ice-cold eggs don't produce the greatest volume, so bring them out of the refrigerator a half-hour before beating. For extra-light-textured muffins, whisk whites and yolks separately.

The recipes in this book use eggs sized as "large," which should give ¼ cup of liquid. If you use "medium" eggs, crack them into a measuring cup and add sufficient cold water to make ¼ cup of liquid, the equivalent of a large egg. When using "jumbo" or "extra large" eggs, crack them into a measuring cup, stir gently to blend the yolk and white, then pour off any egg mixture in excess of ¼ cup; alternatively, reduce the quantity of milk, water or other liquid used in the recipe by this excess amount of egg.

Liquids

The most common liquids used in muffins are milk or water, sometimes a mixture of both; other dairy products can be sour cream, light cream, cottage cheese and nonfat plain or fruit-flavored yogurt.

If you use *raw* (unpasteurized) milk, scald it first, preferably in a double boiler, before adding to the flour, since raw milk contains an organism that destroys the cellular structure of the flour gluten. After scalding raw milk, allow it to cool before adding it to the recipe.

Undiluted *evaporated* milk, straight from the can, will produce a richer muffin. If you dilute evaporated milk with an equal amount of water, it has the same consistency and richness as fresh liquid milk.

If you use canned sweetened *condensed* milk, dilute it with water according to can directions and reduce the amount of sugar in the recipe.

Instant nonfat *dried* milk powder can be successfully used in muffins, mixed with water before adding to the liquid ingredients. To make one cup of reconstituted milk, measure

⅓ cup powder into a liquid-measuring cup and add water to the one-cup level.

When recipes specify *buttermilk* or sour milk and you don't happen to have any on hand, substitute either fresh sweet milk or reconstituted dried milk and add 1 tablespoon lemon juice or mild vinegar to each cup of milk; let it stand a few minutes. Alternatively, canned *powdered buttermilk* is available in health-food stores and large supermarkets; a cup of water and 4 tablespoons of the powder is the equivalent of 1 cup of liquid buttermilk.

If a recipe specifies fresh sweet milk and you only have buttermilk (or your fresh milk has turned sour), reduce by 2 teaspoons the amount of baking powder and replace it with one-half teaspoon baking soda for each cup of buttermilk.

Other liquids used in muffins can be leftover coffee, fruit juices, canned tomato or vegetable juice, vegetable broths and even canned soup and soft tofu. When using the syrup drained from canned fruits as part of the liquid ingredient, cut down or omit the sugar called for in the recipe.

For a touch of ambrosia, substitute up to ¼ cup fruit liqueur for an equal amount of water, then finely chop ½ cup compatible fruit to add to the muffin batter (peach brandy or peach Amaretto with peaches; Chambord liqueur with fresh raspberries; brandy with raisins; coconut liqueur with flaked coconut; Fra Angelico with hazelnuts).

Fats

Quick-breads and muffins generally use larger amounts of fat than yeast breads, since the fat makes the gluten strands more elastic, resulting in muffins that are more tender, flavorful and moist. However you wouldn't want to add too much fat as that makes muffins horribly greasy and overloaded with calories.

Each recipe indicates the particular fat to be used, whether butter, margarine, oil or vegetable shortening. In most cases, it is easier to melt and cool the butter, margarine or shortening and then add it to the other liquid ingredients, but occasionally a recipe will specify that the fat should be cold, cut into fine pieces and rubbed into the flour.

The new-style "Ultralite" muffins substitute fruit purées to replace butter, margarine, vegetable shortening or oil; the amounts of fat have been cut substantially to reduce calories.

Sweetening

Generally, sugar is used in muffins to increase tenderness, improve texture, add flavor and give an attractive color to the crust. To give greater depth of color and distinctive flavor, use sweeteners such as brown sugar, molasses, pure maple syrup, maple sugar or a mild honey, but unless the recipe specifies these alternatives, the results can vary because of the different moisture content. When using molasses, add ½ teaspoon baking soda because of the increased acidity. Even non-sweet savory muffins need a minimal amount of sugar (about 1 or 2 tablespoons) to encourage browning of the crust.

Once you open a box of brown sugar, it can harden very rapidly. Keep it soft by storing in a clean dry glass jar with a few bread crusts and screw the lid down tightly. If brown sugar does harden, remove the lid and zap the sugar with a slice of apple for 30 seconds in the microwave oven.

Herbs

Seasonings of fresh or dried herbs add sparkle and zest to baked savory muffins for particularly good accompaniments to wintry-day soups or summertime salads.

Best of all are herbs freshly picked from your garden or window box. Fresh herbs such as parsley should be trimmed of their woody stems and wilted leaves, then chopped finely. Add to ingredients immediately before spooning batter into muffin wells. Use about 1½ teaspoons for each batch of a dozen muffins.

Dried herbs are at least three times stronger than fresh herbs, so measure accordingly (about ½ teaspoon of herbs such as dried sage, thyme or marjoram). After measuring, place dried herbs in the palm of your hand and rub them with your fingers to release more flavor. Crushed herbs are generally incorporated with the dry flour ingredients before the liquid is added. Store dried herbs in lightproof airproof containers and away from heat. Put date of purchase on tins and toss them out after one year, because after being ground or crushed they quickly lose their special flavors and give disappointing results.

Spices

Sift spices with the flour for even distribution throughout the batter. Additions such as anise, with its delicate licorice flavor, and cardamom are spices associated with Christmas and Easter, but why not use them in every-day muffins and not just for holiday baking? Cinnamon goes well in pumpkin muffins, or as a topping for microwaved muffins that lack a brown crust and come out looking anemic. Ground cloves and ground nutmeg are usually strong and pungent, so use them sparingly, about ¼ teaspoon of either per muffin recipe. Try to buy a whole nutmeg (they can be hard to find in markets, but quality stores stock them) and grate it yourself—the brighter flavor is amazing. Although saffron is the world's most expensive spice, just a pinch or a couple of threads will give a subtle flavor and an attractive golden-yellow tinge to your baking.

Buy ground spices in the smallest packages available, and store in tins or glass jars with tightly fitting lids away from heat and light. After whole spices are ground they immediately begin to lose their strength, so that by the time you reach the bottom of a spice tin, you may need to use more of it. Put purchase dates on the labels and don't keep them for more than one year.

Vanilla and other flavorings

Vanilla beans usually come from Mexico or Madagascar; buy them sealed in glass jars or tightly-wrapped plastic, to be sure of freshness. Look for dark black pods with a slightly "frosty" surface, then place a pod in a jar with sugar reserved for baking, for the aromatic flavor of natural vanilla. Use the sugar to sprinkle on muffin tops and quick-breads after baking. For the simplicity and economy of vanilla in liquid form, shop for quality extract at better grocers or specialty food stores. Some markets also stock easy-to-use vanilla powder: about 1 teaspoon of extract or powder is usually sufficient for each recipe of a dozen muffins.

Check the flavorings shelf in the supermarket for other extracts: almond, coconut, lemon, maple, orange, peppermint or rum.

Nuts and seeds

These additions are high in food value and give a delicious flavor and wonderful crunchy texture to muffins and quickbreads.

Whole nuts should be finely chopped in a nut grinder or a quick spin of a food processor (but not a meat grinder, which makes nuts pasty). If nut pieces are left too large, they may cause the muffins to rise unevenly and break apart irregularly. Nuts and seeds are generally the last ingredients folded gently into the batter before baking. Roughly ½ cup is about the right amount for a recipe for a dozen muffins; too much will weigh down the muffins so they resist rising to their best shape. For microwaved muffins that have no crunchy crust, sprinkle nuts and seeds on top before baking.

Whole seeds such as caraway, cardamom, celery seeds, cumin, fennel, poppy and sesame can all add their distinctive flavors to muffins, either incorporated into the batter or sprinkled on the tops and pressed into the batter just before baking. Fennel has a licorice flavor, much like anise but not so strong. Cumin is a good substitute for caraway. You can buy cardamom as seeds or already crushed to a powder. Crush seeds with a pestle and mortar or use them uncrushed. Generally about ½ to 1½ teaspoons are about the right amount for a twelve-muffin batter.

Fruits, fresh and dried

These additions to muffins give a characteristic flavor and moistness and can be a terrific way to use the bountiful harvests in summer. In winter, toss in drained canned fruits or frozen varieties. They should be finely chopped (whether fresh, canned, or frozen thawed). If fruits are especially juicy they sink to the bottom or make muffins horribly soggy. To avoid this, reserve part of the flour in the recipe; toss the strained fruit with the flour in a small bowl to coat the pieces and absorb some of the juices.

Dried fruit is not limited just to the traditional raisins, sultanas, currants, dates, figs, apricots and prunes. Newcomers include dried cherries (both sweet and sour), apples, pears, peaches and cranberries. Health-food stores often have the most varied selections of dried fruits. When adding dried fruit, you may want to reduce the amount of sugar or other sweeteners in the recipe, to suit your taste.

To cut sticky fruit such as dates, dried apricots, figs, large raisins and glacé cherries, snip them directly into the measuring cup using scissors dipped occasionally in cold water.

For a twelve-muffin recipe using about 2 cups flour, here's a rough guide to the amount of fruit to use:

apple (raw, coarsely grated):	¼ to ½ cup
apricots, peaches, prunes	
(dried, cooked, chopped):	½ to 1 cup
cherries (candied or glacé, chopped):	¼ cup
citron (candied, chopped):	¼ cup
currants (dried):	½ cup
ginger (candied or preserved in syrup,	
well drained and chopped):	½ cup
lemon or orange peel (zest):	1 tablespoon
raisins, dark or light	
(chopped, if large):	½ to 1 cup

Vegetables

You generally need to sauté vegetables such as peeled and chopped onions, garlic or celery in a tiny spoonful of vegetable oil or butter before adding them to the batter. This step breaks down the cellulose walls and releases flavors. Eggplant, carrots and zucchini are generally left unpeeled, grated coarsely and drained well. Half a package of dehydrated onion soup mix can give a delightfully different flavor. Pumpkin is usually cooked, drained and mashed before mixing with liquid ingredients. Leftover cooked vegetables such as asparagus tips and leeks should be drained, then finely diced in order to blend well with the other ingredients.

Garlic-flavored muffins can become a family favorite: peel and finely chop a garlic clove, or measure ½ teaspoon of dried garlic powder, to add a special touch to savory muffins that will partner hearty soups, pastas or vegetarian chile. Garlic also makes a delicious muffin spread when blended into softened butter with a grating of fresh Parmesan cheese.

Sea vegetables

Sea vegetables such as dried wakame strips should be soaked in cold water for about 5 minutes until pliable. Drain, rinse and chop finely. Cook in a little vegetable broth until tender, about 8 minutes. The flavor is delicate.

Just a little extra...

Have fun by inventing your own variations on a basic muffin recipe; play around with other add-ins: crushed pineapple (very well drained), crushed peppermint candies, mini chocolate chips, peanut butter and peanut butter chips. About ½ cup added to a recipe would be about right.

If you add oatmeal, choose the kind that cooks in five to ten minutes rather than overprocessed "instant" or "quick" versions. Up to 1 cup of oatmeal replaces an equal amount of all-purpose flour.

Crushed graham crackers can also replace an equal amount of all-purpose flour. Packaged crumbs are a convenience, but it's easy to crush your own in a food-processor or roll them between two sheets of waxed paper. For 1 cup of crumbs, crush 9 crackers.

Wheat bran, oat bran and bran flake cereals add a grainy texture, but too much bran produces dense, lead-heavy muffins. Up to 1 cup can replace an equal amount of all-purpose flour.

The crowning touch

Although quality muffins are delicious served just the way they come from the oven, it doesn't have to stop there! Many are even more appealing and delectable if you bake on a topping, frost them after baking, or whip up a spread that complements the special ingredients. While some purists may say that this step makes muffins into cupcakes, what does it matter? The results are outstanding and irresistible!

Baked-on toppings

Before slipping the muffins into the oven, glazes and toppings sprinkled and pressed into the batter can give them an attractive look. Here are a few ideas:

+ cinnamon sugar;
+ oatmeal;
+ finely chopped nuts;
+ small seeds such as caraway, celery, flaxseed or poppy;
+ pearl sugar, or hard candy crushed into fine pieces;
+ granola cereal: crush ½ cup granola cereal to reduce any large lumps, and mix with 2 tablespoons melted butter;
+ streusel: combine 2 tablespoons butter, 4 tablespoons brown sugar, 4 tablespoons flour and ½ teaspoon cinnamon.

After-baking frostings

One of the following can give just the right touch of perfection to the beauties you've baked:

Sugar top: Five minutes before end of baking, sprinkle generously with vanilla sugar (sugar that has been stored with a vanilla bean), coarse pearl sugar, or a light dusting of confectioners' sugar.

White frosting: Allow muffins to cool, then spread with frosting: beat together 1 cup sifted confectioners' sugar with 2 tablespoons of either milk, cream, brandy, rum or Sherry. Decorate with toasted sliced almonds, candied cherries, jellied orange slices, M & M candies, or multi-colored sugar confetti, for a festive touch.

Lemon or orange glaze: Prick muffins with the tines of a fork as soon as you bring them from the oven. Drizzle with a glaze made with 1 cup of sifted confectioner's sugar blended with the juice of a lemon or medium orange.

Quick caramel: Drizzle muffins with caramel ice-cream topping.

Marshmallow dreams: Top each muffin with a spoonful of marshmallow creme.

Muffin spreads

Split each muffin horizontally with a sharp knife and spread with one of these:

+ unsalted butter, softened;
+ garlic butter (finely chopped and mashed garlic clove, with a spoonful of freshly grated Parmesan cheese, blended into softened butter);
+ maple butter (pure maple syrup blended into softened unsalted butter);
+ maple-lemon butter (pure maple syrup blended with softened unsalted butter, lemon juice, lemon zest and powdered sugar);
+ honey;
+ honey spice (honey blended with cinnamon and unsalted butter);
+ honey mustard (honey blended into a mild mustard, or already-prepared commercial spread);
+ cream cheese, softened at room temperature and whipped;
+ dressed-up cream cheese, softened at room temperature and whipped with a spoonful of pineapple juice or orange juice;
+ a thin slice of Cheddar cheese (replace top of muffin and reheat in microwave oven for about 30 seconds until cheese melts), good with muffins flavored with chili, herbs or sautéed onions;
+ peanut butter (good with muffins containing raisins or chopped nuts);
+ fruit jellies and jams;
+ fruit preserves and conserves;
+ fruit butters (no fat in these, but a thick concentrate of pure fruit); for example, apple butter (page 182) is an especially good accent with apple muffins, while a pumpkin spread (page 194) goes well with spicy muffins;

+ tangy less-sweet British-style orange marmalade,
   awfully good with orange or lemon muffins;
+ lemon curd (page 108), delicious with lemon or orange
   muffins;
+ guacamole (mashed ripe avocado, thinned with a
   spoonful of mayonnaise, and accented with garlic
   powder, chili powder and cilantro), good with green
   chili muffins and green pepper muffins;
+ salsa (finely chopped tomato, onion, green pepper and
   cilantro), a distinctive spread for cheese muffins.

Nutrition facts

Nutritional values for each recipe have been calculated by
the computer software program "Food Processor 2" from
ESHA Research. Any ingredient values not in the program's
database have been provided by manufacturers or wholesal-
ers of the specific product or food item used. If alternative
ingredients are listed, the first item only is included in figure;
optional ingredients are excluded.

In figuring analyses, several assumptions have been made:
unless otherwise specified, flour is unbleached all-purpose,
butter is salted, oil is canola, eggs are large-size and milk is
nonfat skim.

The analyses don't include percentages of fat since figures
can be misleading when applied to a single recipe rather than
to an entire diet. Nutritionists recommend that fat should be
no more than 30 percent of the *total* calories you consume in a
day—not of each dish or serving.

If you need fat percentages, they are easy to figure: since
each gram of fat (whether butter, margarine, oil or shortening)
contains 9 calories, multiply the number of grams of fat by 9,
then divide by the total number of calories and multiply by
100.

Special diet adjustments

For readers with special diets to follow, alternative ingredients can be used. When making these adjustments, remember
the nutrition analysis provided with each recipe will change.

Vegetarian and Vegan: The recipes contain no meat, fish or poultry, so they fit in beautifully with a vegetarian diet. However, because eggs, milk, cheeses and other dairy products have been used, Vegans will want a few substitutions, such as vegetable margarine instead of butter and nondairy rennet-free cheese or soy cheese instead of dairy cheese. A powdered eggless product can be interchanged for eggs; check packages for directions. Nondairy soy-based substitutes for milk, yogurt and sour cream are available, but for most recipes, soy milk needs thickening with a roux made of flour or cornstarch to produce the consistency of dairy milk. Health-food stores also stock a non-soy milk alternative made of water, almonds and brown rice syrup; non-soy cheese-alternative contains almonds, casein and carrageen. These soy-based items are also helpful for dieters and people who can't eat dairy products.

Chocolate allergy: Substitute carob powder for chocolate. See page 184, Chapter 6.

Egg allergy: For each egg, substitute 1 tablespoon of lecithin, but no more than 2 tablespoons per recipe.

High calorie: In place of milk, use half & half or light cream.

High protein: Substitute ¼ cup raw wheat germ and ¼ cup dried nonfat milk powder for an equal amount of all-purpose flour. Or boost protein with the Cornell formula: to each cup of all-purpose flour add 1 tablespoon raw wheat germ, 1 tablespoon soy flour and 1 tablespoon dried nonfat milk powder.

Lactose intolerance: In place of milk or cream, substitute water, fruit juice, broth, soy milk or a non-soy milk alternative. Some patients can tolerate lowfat yogurt. [Refer to *Osteoporosis: Brittle Bones and the Calcium Crisis* by this author.]

Low calorie: Substitute water or nonfat yogurt for milk or cream. Omit butter, shortening or cooking oil, and replace with equal amount of fruit purée. See "Ultralite" recipes.

Low cholesterol: For each whole egg, use two egg whites or egg substitute (see package instructions). For butter, use soy margarine.

Sodium-free: Either omit salt entirely or substitute potassium chloride. Instead of milk, substitute water. Instead of regular baking powder, substitute an equal quantity of sodium-free baking powder. Several commercial blends are available, but you can quite easily mix your own as follows:

2 tablespoons cream of tartar (potassium bitartrate)
2 tablespoons potassium bicarbonate and
2 tablespoons arrowroot starch.

[Refer to *The Sodium-Watcher's Guide* by this author.]

Wheat or gluten intolerance: This can be a problem because it is the gluten quality in wheat grains that is the key to making muffins tender and light. If your doctor or dietitian has instructed you to avoid wheat, however, you need to substitute rye-, rice-, soy-, tapioca-, or potato-flour, arrowroot, cornflour or buckwheat. Results will be variable and may not be satisfactory as the muffins may be heavy and dense. [Refer to *The Complete Guide to Digestive Health* by this author.]

Chapter 2

Baking Basics: Cool Tools, Hot Tips

Even if your kitchen is only the size of a postage stamp, you probably already have all you need for putting the batter together and producing rave-winning muffins.

Kitchen equipment

The bowls and utensils for making muffins and quick-breads are extremely simple and basic. For most recipes, the following will be handy:

a large bowl (2½ quart to hold the flour and other dry ingredients);

smaller bowls (1½ quart and 1½ pint) for the liquids;

measuring cups (¼ cup to 2 cups):
glass or clear plastic for liquids;
metal or plastic for dry ingredients;

measuring spoons, in 1 tablespoon, and 1, ½ and ¼ teaspoon sizes;

a sieve for flour;

a colander for draining juicy fruit;

a board for chopping fruit or vegetables;

kitchen scissors for snipping dried fruit;

a firm rubber spatula for scooping out that last spoonful of batter from the bowl;

a cake-tester (or a bunch of wooden toothpicks) for checking doneness; and

a wire rack for cooling muffins and quick-breads after baking.

Measure for measure

While some cooks claim they get along fine by merely taking a handful of this and a pinch of that, for consistently good results you need to measure accurately to give yourself the best possible start.

When measuring flour and other dry ingredients, don't just guess: spoon it from the jar or tin into a measuring cup or spoon letting it mound, then level off the top with the straight edge of a knife or spatula. Most brands of flour are pre-sifted so you don't need to sift before measuring. Don't shake the cup to level it as this packs down the flour.

The general rule is never pack dry ingredients. An exception is brown sugar which needs to be packed firmly enough so that the sugar keeps the shape of the measuring cup when it's turned out.

For liquids, place the liquid-measuring cup on a level surface, get your eye level with the mark you want to read and pour the liquid to that line. For easy reading, open an upper cabinet door and place the cup on the shelf nearest eye level.

To measure shortening and peanut butter, use a dry-measuring cup. Pack it down tightly to release air bubbles, then level.

For shredded or grated cheese, nuts or chopped fruit, lightly spoon it into a dry-measuring cup until ingredients are even with the rim but not packed.

For honey and molasses, use liquid-measuring cups lightly coated with vegetable cooking spray, for easy cleanup.

When measuring dried herbs, keep as close as possible to the level of the spoon.

Baking pans

If you have any problems in finding the right pans in local hardware or kitchen equipment stores, refer to Appendix 3 for some useful addresses.

Sizes: Standard pans: wells measure about 2½ or 2¾ inches across the top and hold about one-half cup of batter. Pans with a dozen wells are generally the most useful for families.

Mini-muffin pans: wells measure 1¾ inches across and hold about ¼ cup of batter; muffins from these mini-pans bake fast, have a good crust, and their two-bite size makes them ideal for the buffet table.

Jumbo-size pans: wells measure about 3 inches across and hold about ⅔ cup of batter. These larger muffins will need 5 or 10 minutes longer than standard size to bake.

Fancy cups: for special events or as a change from simple round muffins, buy pans with hearts or other fancifully-shaped wells at kitchen-supply stores or Williams-Sonoma in San Francisco by mail order.

For a whole loaf suitable for slicing, bread pans usually measure:

9 x 5 x 3 inches (6 cups of batter);

8½ x 4½ x 2½ inches (5 cups of batter); and

4¾ x 3¼ x 2¼ inches (2 cups of batter).

For small loaves, suitable for sampler gift breads, use 6 oz fruit juice cans 3½ x 2 inches diameter.

For shallower coffee cakes, cornbreads, etc. to cut into squares and sticks: 8 inches or 9 inches square (6 cups of batter).

Pan materials: Before buying anything, think first of the way you want your muffins to turn out, because it may determine the type of pan material you should shop for. For baking in the conventional oven, pans are made of aluminum, cast iron or glass. (Some readers may have reservations about using aluminum, believing it to be toxic, but by lining wells with paper baking cases, see below, no food comes in contact with the metal.) Metal pans often are given a nonstick finish such as Teflon II™, Silverstone™ or Supra™; muffins come out quickly and cleaning is easy. The surface of the pan determines the amount of browning: a bright shiny aluminum pan produces muffins with a light golden-brown crust, top and bottom; pans with dark, rough, dull finishes, or made of colored or clear glass absorb heat, resulting in muffins with a browner, crisper crust.

Cast-iron pans may hold slightly less batter than pans of other materials, but they produce crustier muffins that stand higher. Corn-stick molds, usually made of cast iron, make crusty corn-sticks about 5 inches long.

Cast iron should be "seasoned" before use, to make clean-

ing easier and prevent rusting: to season, coat the inside sur-
faces with cooking oil or vegetable shortening, then heat the
pan in a 250 degree F. oven for two hours. When cool, wipe
away the excess oil or shortening. Reseason when foods later
begin to stick to the pan.

Season new glass pans or custard cups by greasing them
and placing in a 350 degree F. oven for 30 minutes. Remove
grease then regrease cups or spray them with a nonstick cooking spray before using. When baking with clear or colored
glass cups, reduce the recommended oven temperature by 25
degrees F.

For microwave baking, *never* use metal pans: pans specially
designed for use in the microwave oven are made of plastic,
and usually have 6 wells containing 3 cups of batter.

Cup liners: Using liners is a matter of personal choice: they
eliminate the need to grease the muffin wells, but not everyone cares to peel the paper off the muffins after baking. However, you can get a pretty effect by lining muffin wells with
paper cases and even ice-cream cones. Paper cases come in
classic white, pastel-colored, printed with holiday motifs such
as holly, or have an outer case of silver or gold foil. When
baking muffins in the microwave, line each well of the microwave-safe muffin pan with *two* paper liners, for extra strength
(but never use the *foil* type of liners in the microwave).

Place ice-cream cones with flat bottoms in muffin wells to
make edible cases for baking in the conventional oven, not the
microwave. Fill with batter to within one inch of cone tops.
Bake at once, so that cones remain crisp. If not baked immediately after filling, the batter makes cones limp and soggy.

Nonstick cooking spray is ideal for lowfat baking. The
spray is a light vegetable oil. Be sure to work over the sink
when coating pans: accidental overspray of oil on countertops
results in a mess; oil on the floor can cause slippery accidents.

Baking tips

Before we begin baking, let's go over a few important
points about muffin-making so that you can be sure of success
every time. Whether your muffin wells are mini, middy or
maxi, the preparation method is the same.

✦ Muffins and quick-breads don't need the kneading and proofing that's necessary with yeast breads.

✦ Before beginning to prepare a recipe, get organized: assemble all the ingredients, measuring utensils, bowls and muffin tins or loaf pans on your kitchen counter or table.

✦ Prepare baking pans by lining with waxed-paper muffin cases or cones. If you like really crusty muffins, skip this step and spray each well with nonstick cooking spray or grease thoroughly with hard shortening. Muffins often stick obstinately in their wells when butter or oil is used (although butter can impart a delicious subtle flavor). Teflon pans need not be greased.

✦ Don't guess at ingredients' measures. Read through all recipe directions before you start so you know what to expect, then follow closely. Although measures are given exactly, remember that flours vary in moisture content and will absorb liquid ingredients accordingly, so you may need to make adjustments.

✦ Sifting the baking powder and dry ingredients together after measuring distributes them evenly through the flour, helping to give a good texture.

✦ Easy does it. Repeat after me: *don't over-beat*. The ideal batter for muffins and quick-breads should be gently stirred only until the flour is blended in and the dough soft. Don't worry that the batter may be lumpy—the ingredients will carry on blending during baking. This will produce great-looking rounded muffins that are tender inside and tunnel-free. A food processor or electric mixer, though wonderful equipment for yeast breads, makes muffin batter too smooth. This is a sign of over-processing, which will result in a disappointing finished product: muffins will be weirdly pointed and filled with tunnels. If you want to beat the egg thoroughly and blend liquid ingredients with a processor, go ahead, but when working the liquids into the flour and dry ingredients, you need the light touch and gentleness of hand-stirring.

✦ Muffin batter should be very soft—not runny and not stiff. If batter is too thin, sprinkle in an extra tablespoon of flour. If too stiff, add a spoonful more of the liquid called for.

✦ High altitudes: if you live at a high elevation, you may need a few adjustments to recipes. See box.

Tips for high living

The muffin recipes in this guide have been tested for baking at sea level; they need no modification up to an altitude of 3,000 feet (for metric equivalents, refer to Appendix 2). If you live higher than that, decreased atmospheric pressure and an increased evaporation rate may cause too much rising and a weakened batter mixture. You can avoid this by reducing amounts of baking powder and sugar, and increasing the amount of liquid. It also helps to increase the oven temperature by 25 degrees F. to "set" the muffin batter before it expands too much. The following is a rough guide to the adjustments you need:

Adjustment	*3,000ft*	*5,000ft*	*7,000ft*
Baking powder: for each tsp, *cut by:*	⅛ tsp	⅛ to ¼ tsp	¼ tsp
Sugar: for each cup, *cut by:*	1 tbsp	1 to 2 tbsp	1 to 3 tbsp
Liquid: for each cup, *add:*	1 to 2 tbsp	2 to 4 tbsp	3 to 4 tbsp

Use the smaller adjustment first, and experiment several times with each recipe until you find the most successful proportions that work at your altitude. For more information on baking at high elevations, write to Colorado State University Cooperative Extension, Fort Collins, Colorado 80523, for *High Altitude Food Preparation Pamphlet 41.*

✦ Oven temperatures for muffins generally range between 350 and 400 degrees F. for between 20 to 30 minutes. Quick-bread loaves usually need between 325 and 350 degrees F. for between 50 minutes and 1¼ hours. If you try several recipes and they aren't successful, maybe your oven temperature is incorrect. As ranges and wall ovens get older, it's not uncommon for the temperature to shift. Check it with an oven thermometer available at hardware or kitchen supply stores.

✦ Fill wells about two-thirds full (but only half full when microwaving, as they usually double in volume).

✦ Place the oven shelf in the middle of the oven, not the top or bottom levels, since temperatures can vary by as much as 25 to 30 degrees F., depending on the position of your heat source. Don't change racks when the oven is hot—you can get a bad burn.

✦ If leavening in the recipe is baking *soda,* reaction with liquid is almost instantaneous, so you need a preheated oven for immediate baking after you've filled the wells. For baking-*powder* muffins you can heat the oven *after* you've prepared the batter mixture and are ready to spoon it into the muffin wells. Waiting for the oven to reach the correct temperature allows time for the baking powder to act with the liquid and flour, for a headstart on the leavening process before the muffins feel the oven heat.

✦ Medium-sized muffins generally take about 20 to 30 minutes to bake, mini-muffins 15 to 20 minutes, jumbos about 40 minutes, and loaf-size usually need 1 hour to 1¼ hours. Don't be tempted to open the oven door for a peek until the minimum time has elapsed. Take care to close the door gently if you resume baking—slamming the door shut causes a draft that makes the temperature vary.

✦ Check muffins for doneness: see if tops are turning brown (except savory muffins, which contain less sugar). Quickbreads will begin to pull their sides slightly away from the loaf pan. A cake tester or toothpick probed into the middle should come out clean. If it's still squishy, try five minutes more. Another test is to lightly press a finger to the tops; they should give slightly—resilient but tender. If they feel firm, you've over-baked.

✦ Muffins and quick-breads leavened with baking powder or soda very often develop cracks across the top—but don't worry as they're quite typical and the muffins should still have a lovely even texture inside. If you'd rather see a neat crack, score across the top of the batter of each muffin or loaf with a sharp knife before slipping them into the oven, to give a professional touch.

✦ Allow muffins to cool slightly in their pans for 5 to 10 minutes, quick-bread loaves 15 minutes, before removing them to a wire rack. Serve muffins while still warm; slice noyeast loaves the following day when they are less crumbly.

✦ Muffins and quick-breads store beautifully in the freezer if you wrap them well. Either make a package of aluminum foil, with the foil pressed firmly but gently against them to block out air; or place muffins in a plastic bag, close bag tightly, and seal well. Then put this bag inside another plastic bag. Using the double-bag method, breads and muffins keep for up to three months. Label and date the package before freezing.

✦ Reheat thawed muffins wrapped in foil in a conventional oven for about 15 minutes at 350 degrees F. Individual muffins in paper cases will reheat in a microwave oven in about 1 minute each, at full power (but overheating in the microwave can toughen them).

✦ If you follow directions carefully and still get weird results—don't worry! Refer to Appendix 1 for problems and their possible causes, then try the recipe again.

✦ Microwaving: The microwave is a time-saver for melting butter, softening cream cheese or hard brown sugar, plumping raisins or dried fruit, melting paper-wrapped baking chocolate or chocolate chips, and toasting nuts or flaked coconut. Muffins *can* be baked in a microwave oven, but this is not a preferred method. They're usually unattractive because they tend to remain too wet on the outside; they don't develop a crust or turn brown (unless your oven has a convection setting for browning). But they do bake quickly if you're in a real hurry—you can microwave them while the coffee is brewing. Six microwaved muffins, in microwave-suitable plastic pans, take only 2 to 3 minutes to bake, or until muffins no longer look doughy and only the surface is wet. (See box on next page for testing microwave wattage). Rotate after one minute (don't over-bake or you'll end up with cannon balls!). If muffins are not done, add time in 30-second intervals. Remove immediately from pan and cool 5 minutes on the countertop, to let muffins finish cooking as they sit on the flat surface.

✦ To make muffins look more appealing after microwaving, you can conceal the pale color with a top sprinkling of cinnamon sugar or frosting or, for savory muffins, a dusting of paprika. When muffins lack a crust, a topping of chopped nuts or small seeds such as poppy or flaxseed will add crunchiness. Because microwaving batter doesn't form

---

What about...
the wattage of your microwave oven?

Muffins take 2 to 3 minutes to bake in a 700-watt microwave oven; with lower-wattage ovens, foods take a little longer. Here's a test:

1. Fill a glass measuring cup with 1 cup of cold water.
2. Place cup in center of oven and heat the water on HIGH.
3. How much time did it take for the water to reach a rolling boil?

2½ to 3 minutes? your oven has	600 to 700 watts
3 to 3½ minutes?	500 to 600 watts
3½ to 4 minutes?	400 to 500 watts
4½ to 5½ minutes?	300 to 400 watts

---

a crust during cooking, muffins tend to dry out more quickly than those baked in a conventional oven, but you can retain moisture with toppings, frostings and glazes. They are best served on the day you make them.

✦ Present your baked muffins in an attractive basket or wooden bowl covered with a soft linen cloth. For a special buffet, tuck small fresh flowers around the base of the basket for a splash of color.

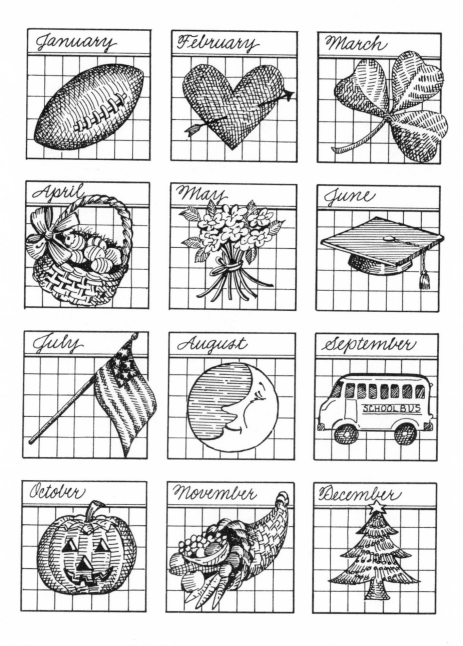

Chapter 3

Muffin of the Month

Some cooks can skillfully improvise, never write anything down and never look at a recipe. But recipes are to cooks what road maps are to drivers, and we all need directions and help when striking out for what may be unknown territory.

This personal collection of favorite muffins and quick-breads is presented in four chapters: Muffin of the Month, Sweet and Easy, Savory Specials, and the contemporary-styled "Ultralites" with little or no fat and a reduced number of calories.

The non-recipes on even-numbered pages give hints and history, essays and anecdotes, facts and fables, aiming to amuse, inform or entertain armchair cooks and non-cooking readers.

Muffin of the Month includes what might be called a merry-go-round with the calendar reflecting our rich heritage, varied customs and cultures—tracing traditions, events, celebrations, fiestas, festivals and fun-making throughout the year, giving you inspiration and opportunities for plenty of muffin baking. Let's start cooking!

January: Football!

The pastime of kicking around a ball goes back before recorded history, as even ancient peoples played football in a primitive way. Around 2,500 years ago, Athenians, Spartans and Corinthians were playing a ball-kicking game which the Greeks called *Episkuros*. To the Romans the game was known as *Harpastum*, which they took with them when they invaded Britain in the first century B.C.

Until 1823, the game played in the British Isles was soccer (Association Football), in which running with the ball is not allowed. However, in that year, a defiant English schoolboy named William Webb Ellis took it into his head to run with the ball during a game at Rugby School. Thereafter, two separate football-type games have been played in Britain—soccer and Rugby.

U.S. football has its origins in the British game of Rugby, although Americans altered the rules and style, and made many modifications over the years. No particular skill was needed and no rules applied: originally it was a no-holds-barred game played in any convenient field. Over a century ago, informal football was played on college lawns. During the late 19th century, teams consisted of 25, 20, 15 or 11 men to a side, with the play rough and brutal—piling on, hurdling and hair-pulling were all part of the game in the 1880s. Then in 1906 President Theodore Roosevelt held a meeting at the White House with representatives from Yale, Harvard and Princeton, when they agreed to modify rules for a faster and cleaner game.

And what about the Super Bowl? The first was played on January 15, 1967, at the Los Angeles Coliseum between the Green Bay Packers of the National Football League and the Kansas City Chiefs of the American Football League.

Today's play has evolved into a complex game though still a rough-house—but at least the teams now wear protective helmets and pads as they tear into each other.

Super-Bowl Blue-Cheese Muffins

The formal parties of the holiday season are over, but January kicks off with events such as New Year's Day football and the Super Bowl when you want to cook in more casual fashion but still bring superb food to the buffet table or the tailgate picnic. With pre-game preparation of steaming casseroles of hearty chili thick with beans and vegetables, big bowls of tossed green salads, a selection of dressings on the sideline, and a basket of zesty golden-domed cheese-flecked muffins as a team-mate, you won't miss any of the action on field.

2 cups unbleached all-purpose flour
2 teaspoons baking powder
½ teaspoon dry English mustard
2 tablespoons granulated sugar
1 large egg
1 cup nonfat skim milk
¼ cup (½ stick) melted butter or soy margarine
¼ cup crumbled blue cheese
¼ cup grated sharp Cheddar cheese

Coat muffin wells with nonstick cooking spray.

In a 2½ quart mixing bowl, sift together the flour, baking powder, mustard and sugar. Stir to blend and make a well in center.

In a 1½ quart bowl, whisk the egg, milk and melted butter. Stir egg mixture into the flour mixture, then add cheeses. Stir only until combined; batter should remain slightly lumpy. Spoon batter into prepared wells until two-thirds full.

Bake in a preheated oven at 400 degrees F. for 25 minutes or until golden brown. Turn onto wire rack.

Makes about 12 2½" muffins.

Each muffin contains about: 150 calories, 4.5g protein, 19g carbohydrate, .5g fiber, 6g fat, 33mg cholesterol, 157mg sodium.

February: Valentine's Day

Although February puts on the calendar Groundhog Day, Presidents' birthdays and Mardi Gras, the month is dominated by Valentine's Day—the busiest time for florists, card shops and candy stores.

One legend tells how the holiday on February 14 began when Valentinus, a third century Roman priest and physician, was martyred for refusing to give up Christianity. Just before he was executed, he passed a note to the jailer's daughter whom he'd befriended in prison, and signed it "from your Valentine."

A European belief of the Middle Ages suggested that the day was related to the mating time of birds, so lovers should also exchange messages and notes on that date. In *Parlement of Foules*, Chaucer mentions:

For this was Seynt Valentine's Day,
When every foul [fowl] cometh ther to choose his mate.

The paper valentine, decorated with lace, hearts and flowers, lovers' knots and Cupids, was probably the first of all greeting cards, dating from the sixteenth century as a special affectionate message of love. By the 1780s, printed cards were becoming common, especially in Germany, where they were known as *Freundschaftkarten* or "friendship cards."

The heart shapes that appear on sentimental valentines have been symbols of love for centuries, although they would not be recognized by cardiologists! Researchers have speculated about the origin: was it an imprint that might remain on paper when kissed by milady's rouged lips? or a shapely woman with generous breasts and nipped-in waist?

The lovers' festival has long been the time for sweethearts to exchange sweets as well as sweet messages. But for food lovers, Valentine's Day arrives at an unfortunate time of year; just when you are about to tackle the diet you vowed on January 1, along comes a red satin box of Valentine candy!

Cherry Pink Affairs

These romantic pink-tinged muffins are more meaningful than a box of candy, and express love in the tenderest way possible; your sweetheart can't fail to get the right message. Delicious romance! Create the right mood by setting the table with china, napkins and flowers all in shades of blush.

1¾ cups unbleached all-purpose flour
2 teaspoons baking powder
½ teaspoon salt
⅓ cup granulated sugar
1 (9-oz) jar maraschino cherries
½ cup maraschino-cherry juice (from cherry jar)
1 large egg
¼ cup nonfat skim milk
¼ cup (½ stick) melted butter or soy margarine
Frosting (optional), see below

Line muffin wells with pink and white paper cases (or for a charming touch, use heart-shaped muffin pans).

Sift together the dry ingredients in a 2½ quart mixing bowl, stir to blend and make a well in center.

Drain cherries, reserving juice. Finely chop and measure cherries (should be ¾ cup).

In a 1½ quart bowl, whisk egg, cherry juice, milk and melted butter. Pour egg mixture into dry ingredients and stir until just moistened. Gently fold in chopped cherries. Spoon batter into prepared muffin wells.

Bake in a preheated oven at 400 degrees F. for 15 to 20 minutes until muffins are delicately brown and a test toothpick comes out clean. Serve warm with love.

For the lover with a sweet tooth, cool muffins for a few minutes then coat tops with a simple frosting as follows: ½ cup confectioners' sugar blended with remaining maraschino cherry juice and a drop or two of almond extract. Beat until smooth.

Makes about 12 2½" muffins.

Each muffin (without frosting) contains about: 163 calories, 3g protein, 29g carbohydrate, .5g fiber, 4.5g fat, 28mg cholesterol, 191mg sodium.

March: St. Patrick's Day

'Tis a great day for the Irish when St. Patrick's Day arrives! It's a time when everybody becomes a little bit Irish, even if they've never been to Ireland: they'll wear something green, march in a parade and handle a mug of green beer. About 40 million Americans claim Irish roots.

Patrick was not born in Ireland. Where then? Some say Dumbarton, Scotland, or in Glastonbury in Monmouthshire, Tours in France, or in Wales, in the fourth century A.D. At the age of sixteen he was captured by Irish raiders and sold as a slave to a Druid chief in what is now County Antrim, Ireland. When he was twenty-two, Patrick decided to devote his life to religion, spending eighteen years in French monasteries studying to be a priest and later a bishop. Pope Celestine I named him Patricius in the year 431 and sent him to Ireland on a missionary journey to convert pagans, much to the resentment of the Druid priests who regarded his landing as an invasion.

Because many legends have sprung up in connection with St. Patrick's life, works and miracles, it's difficult to separate myth from truth: raising people from the dead, kindling fire from snow, driving the snakes out of Ireland, and preaching to his followers about the Holy Trinity illustrating his sermon by using the leaves of the shamrock that grows abundantly in the country.

One point is clear today: tons of shamrock plants with "a bit of the auld soil clinging to them," are flown across the Atlantic and indeed all over the world each year in time for March 17, so that millions can be "wearin' of the green."

And of course there'll be a parade: wherever Irish gather you can be sure of one! For many blocks along Fifth Avenue in New York, the famous street is packed with more than a million people to watch a hundred thirty thousand Irish—or semi-Irish—marching along the avenue in front of St. Patrick's Cathedral. Pipe-bands, mounted police and social organizations are bursting with Irish pride, in commemoration of the saint who died on March 17 in the year 493.

Irish Coffee Muffins

In spite of the numerous tales that surround the life of St. Patrick, there appears to be no record whatsoever that he ever ate muffins; but the saint would have found it hard to resist these rich coffee-flavored temptations with their heavenly aroma. They can be a special treat for brunch, and are perfect partners for a cup of coffee (straight or spirited) after a St. Patrick's Day dinner.

2 cups unbleached all-purpose flour
2 teaspoons baking powder
½ teaspoon salt
⅓ cup granulated sugar
1 tablespoon instant coffee granules, 2 tablespoons *each*
    coffee liqueur and Irish whiskey, plus milk to
    measure 1 cup
1 large egg
½ cup (1 stick) melted butter or soy margarine
Whipped cream for garnish (optional)

Line muffin wells with paper cases.

In a 2½ quart mixing bowl sift flour, baking powder, salt and sugar, stir to blend and make a well in center.

In a 1-cup measure, dissolve coffee granules with coffee liqueur and whiskey, then top up with milk (if you prefer no spirits, substitute ¼ cup of strong coffee). Whisk egg in a 1½ quart bowl, add liqueur-milk mixture and melted butter. Gently stir liquid mixture into flour mixture until flour is just moistened. Spoon into prepared muffin wells.

Bake in a preheated oven at 375 degrees F. for 25 minutes or until a rich brown. After cooling on a wire rack, serve the muffins split and spread with whipped cream garnish if desired.

Makes about 12 2½" muffins.

Each muffin (without whipped cream) contains about: 194 calories, 3g protein, 24g carbohydrate, .5g fiber, 8g fat, 39mg cholesterol, 236mg sodium.

April: Easter

Easter is one of the happiest holidays of the year and the holiest religious festival in Christian lands, commemorating the Resurrection. It's also a joyous mixture of many secular customs dating from ancient fertility symbols and rites (some traceable to Eostra, the pagan goddess of both dawn and spring): sunrise services, the Easter Bunny, decorated Easter baskets, baby chicks, fresh spring flowers especially lilies, new clothes and Easter bonnets displayed in street parades, chocolate eggs, egg-dyeing, egg-rolling and egg-hunts.

One of the oldest Good Friday customs is the eating of hot cross buns. In early Christian times, the buns were flat and unleavened in imitation of Passover bread eaten by Jesus, but later they were baked from the same dough used in making the Host. But these small sweet buns may have originated in pre-Christian times in ancient Egypt, Greece and the Roman Empire: Egyptians stamped symbolic horns on small loaves baked in Spring in their pagan worship of Isis, the Mother Goddess; ancient Greeks cross-marked cakes as a ritual offering to Diana; and in the Roman city of Herculaneum near Pompeii, archeologists have found two whole loaves each marked with the familiar cross. Early missionaries sent from Rome to Britain blessed the cakes made by Anglo Saxons by drawing a cross upon them.

The custom of "crossing" one's food as a sign of blessing was widespread in Catholic countries in the Middle Ages, the cross being imprinted on bread before baking. The sweet buns have always been extremely popular in Britain, marked after baking with a cross of white icing, on sale in bakers' shops just prior to Good Friday morning or sold by sellers walking through the town streets with their cries of—

Hot cross buns! Hot cross buns!
One a penny, two a penny, hot cross buns!
If you have no daughters, give them to your sons.
One a penny, two a penny, hot cross buns!
If you have no penny, a ha'penny will do.
If you have no ha'penny, God bless you!

Hot Cross Muffins

Although by tradition hot cross buns are made with a yeast leavening, there's no rule against baking powder.

1 cup nonfat skim milk
1 teaspoon saffron threads
1 ⅞ cups unbleached all-purpose flour
2 teaspoons baking powder
½ teaspoon salt
½ cup granulated sugar
1 large egg
¼ cup (½ stick) melted butter or soy margarine
2 teaspoons vanilla extract
½ cup dried currants
½ cup confectioners' sugar

Line muffin wells with paper cases.

Combine 2 tablespoons of the milk with saffron threads in a small saucepan. Heat and stir just to simmering. Remove from heat, add remainder of milk then set aside to cool.

In a 2½ quart bowl sift together flour, baking powder, salt and sugar, stir to blend and make a well in center.

In a 1½ quart bowl whisk egg with milk/saffron mixture, melted butter and 1 teaspoon of the vanilla extract. Add egg mixture to dry ingredients and stir lightly until just blended. Toss in currants and mix. Spoon batter into prepared muffin wells until two-thirds full.

Bake in a preheated oven at 400 degrees F. for 15 to 20 minutes, until golden brown and a test toothpick comes out clean. Allow to cool.

In a small bowl sift confectioners' sugar and blend in remaining teaspoon vanilla extract and sufficient water to make a smooth frosting. Beat well until silky, then paint a simple cross on each muffin.

Makes about 12 2½" muffins.

Each muffin (including cross) contains about: 184 calories, 3.5g protein, 33g carbohydrate, 1g fiber, 4.5g fat, 28mg cholesterol, 199mg sodium.

May: Mother's Day

The merry month of May brings us the ancient celebration of May Day on the 1st, Memorial Day at the end of the month, and then of course Mother's Day on the second Sunday.

Although May Day is not prominently celebrated in America, it is or has been one of the principal festivals in other parts of the world, probably dating back to prehistoric times when it marked the unofficial beginning of Spring, the start of the planting season and the new growth of trees in Northern Europe. At the beginning of May, a popular Roman festival was devoted to the worship of Flora, the goddess of flowers, and many countries still celebrate by dancing around flower-decorated maypoles, in customs traced back to tree worship.

The most significant tradition celebrated with flowers in the United States during May is Mother's Day. Although you may think that a day honoring motherhood also originated in prehistoric times, the observance only dates back to the early part of the twentieth century. (While it's true that "Mothering Sunday" on the fourth Sunday in Lent was a part of the Church calendar for centuries, this was a date to venerate Mary, Mother of God, when parishioners went to the mother church of their parish, laden with offerings.)

On May 10, 1908 a church in Grafton, West Virginia held a memorial service at the request of a Miss Anna M. Jarvis in honor of her own mother, Anna Reese Jarvis. On her instructions, large jars of white carnations (her mother's favorite flower) were set about the church platform. Since then, white carnations have been a sign that one's mother has died, while red ones have symbolized a living mother. In May 1913 it was officially proclaimed that all officials of the federal government and members of both Houses in Washington should wear a carnation on Mother's Day, the second Sunday in May, designated "as a public expression of our love and reverence for the mothers of our country."

What was begun as a religious service has now grown into a popular and happy event commemorated with flowers, gifts and festive dining, not only for mothers but also for grandmothers, aunts, sisters and sweethearts.

Fresh Strawberry Muffins

This is a lovely opportunity to fête mother with a special high-tea featuring these moist and tender muffins, delicately aromatic with fresh fruit. Set a lace-covered tea-table with your finest teapot and china, flanked by a sparkling crystal vase of red carnations. Serve an assortment of pinwheel sandwiches, miniature lemon tartlets, shortbread fingers, and the strawberry muffins along with strawberry preserves. Offer a choice of Darjeeling tea with thin lemon slices or an herbal or lemon tea.

¾ cup finely diced strawberries (slightly under-ripe and firm)
2 cups unbleached all-purpose flour
2 teaspoons baking powder
½ teaspoon baking soda
½ cup granulated sugar
1 cup freshly squeezed orange juice
¼ teaspoon almond extract
1 large egg
¼ cup (½ stick) melted butter or soy margarine

Position rack in center of oven, preheat oven to 400 degrees F. and line muffin wells with paper cases.

In a 1½ pint bowl gently toss the diced strawberries with ½ cup of the flour and set aside.

In a 2½ quart bowl sift remaining 1½ cups of flour with baking powder, baking soda and sugar. Stir in coated strawberries and make a well in center.

In a 1½ quart bowl whisk orange juice, almond extract, egg and melted butter. Beat thoroughly. Pour all at once into the flour mixture and gently fold together. Spoon into prepared muffin wells.

Bake at 400 degrees F. for 20 to 25 minutes or until golden brown.

Makes about 12 2½" muffins.

Each muffin contains about: 161 calories, 3g protein, 27g carbohydrate, 1g fiber, 4.5g fat, 28mg cholesterol, 134mg sodium.

June:
Brides, Grads and Dads

This is a full month for celebrations and memorable occasions—for bridal showers, rehearsal dinners and wedding parties; family gatherings honor father; special dinners celebrate graduation and relief that classes are over.

Countless couples stand before altars to pledge their love for one another and begin new lives together, starting with traditional ceremonies and ancient rituals. The preference for June weddings may go back as far as Roman times, because Juno was the Roman goddess of marriage who presided over this month in the Julian calendar that was considered lucky for weddings. On the other hand, June could also be a popular month for marriage merely because the weather is generally better for honeymoons!

For honored graduates, names are called, diplomas conferred with vigorous handshakes, and the flock of tasseled mortarboards tossed into the air with abandon is a graphic expression of freedom from classes! Graduation ceremonies are followed by special dinners, for restoring students after weeks of cramming and exams. The caps and gowns worn by high school and college students at graduation today are survivors of the everyday dress of scholars of medieval Europe regulated by the church of the Middle Ages.

And then there's dear old dad! Father's Day seems to have started almost as an afterthought to Mother's Day. Although mothers were fêted with flowers and festivities years earlier, fathers apparently weren't *officially* recognized until more recently. The even footing with mothers was slow in coming. It wasn't until 1972 that the third Sunday in June was established permanently when President Nixon signed a Congressional resolution. Father's Day has now become another happy occasion for family dinners and gatherings to honor not only dad but also granddads, uncles, brothers, sons, other relatives and friends.

Chocolate Orange Muffins

Chocolate is an all-round favorite flavor, so it's only natural to include it for the month of June. Dark and rich with chocolate, moist and sweet with mandarin oranges, these top-class muffins will be winners for all your entertaining.

1 (11-oz) can mandarin orange segments
1 ¾ cups unbleached all-purpose flour
1 teaspoon baking soda
½ teaspoon salt
1 tablespoon dried granulated orange peel
½ cup granulated sugar
½ cup unsweetened cocoa powder
1 large egg
1 tablespoon mild vinegar in 1 cup nonfat skim milk
⅓ cup vegetable oil

Position rack in center of oven, preheat oven to 400 degrees F., and line muffin wells with paper cases.

Thoroughly drain orange segments and discard syrup. Measure oranges to make ¾ cup, chop finely and set aside.

In a 2½ quart mixing bowl sift flour, baking soda, salt, orange peel, sugar and cocoa powder. Stir lightly to blend and make a well in the center.

In a 1½ quart bowl whisk egg, vinegar/milk mixture and vegetable oil; beat thoroughly. Stir into flour mixture until just blended. Add drained oranges to batter. Spoon quickly into prepared muffin wells.

Bake at 400 degrees F. for 20 to 25 minutes. Cool 5 minutes before turning out onto a wire rack.

Makes about 12 2½" muffins.

Each muffin contains about: 185 calories, 4g protein, 28g carbohydrate, 2g fiber, 7g fat, 18mg cholesterol, 200mg sodium.

July: The Fourth

No holiday is more American than July 4, the proud celebration of independence: the flag-waving, fireworks and food; the parades, picnics and parties.

Little has changed since John Adams wrote in 1776 that the day should be "solemnized with pomp and parade, with shows, games and sport, guns, bells, bonfires and illuminations..." Although the formal oratory has all but disappeared from the occasion, we still commemorate Independence Day in high spirits similar to those of over two hundred years ago.

The central motif for the holiday is, of course, the "star-spangled banner." Although the legend persists that Betsy Ross sewed the first flag to result from the resolution of the Continental Congress, most scholars discredit the tale. Betsy was undoubtedly a fine seamstress who conducted an upholstery business that included flag-stitching, but Congressional records show no commission being selected to provide a flag. In 1818, however, Congress passed the New Flag Act which set the number of stripes at thirteen, the stars at twenty, and allowed additional stars as new States were admitted to the Union. This Act is still in effect, and under it the stars of Alaska and Hawaii were added in 1959 and 1960 after their admission as States.

No foods could be more American for July 4 than muffins filled with ripe blueberries and spiked with ground allspice. The blueberry comes from a native North American shrub, now mainly cultivated in the acidic soils of northern States as well as Canada. Commercial quantities are also picked from wild plants which generally bear small-sized fruit with a more intense concentrated flavor.

Allspice is an aromatic berry from a tropical American native with the pungent flavor that suggests a mixture of cinnamon, cloves and nutmeg, but unlike those other spices it is derived from the Western Hemisphere, from trees cultivated in dense hillside plantations in the West Indies, Mexico and Central America.

All-American Muffins

For entertaining with style, have food and accompaniments that everyone is familiar with—nothing fancy or intimidating. A buffet of light fare is just the right accent for the day, so that friends and family feel free to take as much or as little as they want; just make sure there's plenty, and keep everything relaxed and casual.

You may want to make a double batch of muffins ahead of time. They freeze well when tightly wrapped in aluminum foil; reheat them at the start of your party, for effortless entertaining.

1 cup fresh or frozen (unsweetened) blueberries
1⅞ cups unbleached all-purpose flour
3 teaspoons baking powder
½ teaspoon salt
1 teaspoon ground allspice
¼ cup granulated sugar
1 large egg
1 cup nonfat skim milk
¼ cup (½ stick) melted butter or soy margarine

Line muffin wells with paper cases. Wash blueberries in a colander and blot dry with paper towel. In a small bowl toss berries with ½ cup of the flour, then set aside.

In a 2½ quart bowl sift remaining flour with baking powder, salt, allspice and sugar. Stir to blend and make a well in center.

In a 1½ quart bowl whisk egg, milk and butter and add all at once to the flour mixture. Stir lightly until flour is moistened, then fold in floured berries. Spoon batter into prepared muffin wells, until two-thirds full.

Bake in a preheated oven at 400 degrees F. for about 20 minutes until golden brown and a test toothpick in center comes out clean. Do not over-bake.

Makes about 12 2½" muffins.

Each muffin contains about: 143 calories, 3g protein, 22g carbohydrate, 1g fiber, 4.5g fat, 28mg cholesterol, 227mg sodium.

August:
The Chinese Moon Festival

Americans enjoy summertime barbecues in backyards, parks and beaches, but another type of festival is celebrated outdoors as the full moon rises in the Orient—with lighted candles and incense sticks, banging gongs and crashing cymbals. Moon-cakes and hot rice wine typify the Moon Festival, a major three-day Chinese holiday that comes at the eighth full moon of the Lunar Year, marking the time when summer heat gives way to autumn coolness, and summer brightness to winter darkness. Banqueting celebrants sip rice wine, recite their own poems or those of classic Chinese poets, and feast at midnight when the moon is brightest.

Days before, the shops are full of special cakes and toys, everyone fervently hoping that the celebration will not be marred by cloudy weather, since the Moon Festival takes place outdoors, where people give moon-viewing parties—and the essential festival gift is a box of four moon-cakes bought at bakeries.

Moon-cakes, unlike most Chinese dainties, are sweet, especially in southern provinces where sugar is plentiful. They are always baked of a gray ("moon-colored") flour to make a lightly-sweetened flaky biscuit dough, and look like deep, covered pies, glazed with a shiny egg-wash and embossed with a red sign of double happiness. Fillings are various: sweet bean or date paste, pineapple and raisins, coconut and pine nuts, walnuts or whatever other nuts and fruits are available, or a salted duck-egg yolk at their center to represent the moon.

Many Chinese women prefer to bake moon-cakes at home as an act of piety, and stuff them extravagantly if they can afford it. With deep bows to an outdoor altar in the family shrine, the women arrange their moon-cakes in a pyramid of thirteen to symbolize the number of months in the Chinese year and a complete "circle of happiness" for family unity.

Moon-Cake Muffins

Although these moon-cake muffins were inspired by Chinese moon-cakes, they aren't intended to be replicas of those Oriental sweet delicacies. At the same time, using slices of jade-colored round-shaped kiwifruit (Chinese gooseberries) for the filling is meant to represent the full moon; the delicate red topping conveys happiness.

1 medium kiwifruit, peeled
1⅞ cups unbleached all-purpose flour
2 teaspoons baking powder
½ teaspoon ground ginger
½ cup granulated sugar, plus 2 tablespoons for topping
2 large eggs
¼ cup (½ stick) melted butter or soy margarine
1 cup nonfat skim milk
Few drops red food coloring

Position rack in center of oven, preheat oven to 400 degrees F., and coat muffin wells with nonstick cooking spray.

On a chopping board, cut the kiwifruit into 12 thin slices then set aside.

In a 2½ quart bowl sift flour, baking powder, ginger and ½ cup sugar. Stir to blend and make a well in the center.

In a 1½ quart bowl whisk eggs, butter and milk then pour all at once into the flour mixture; stir only until blended.

Spoon batter into muffin wells until only *half* full. Carefully place one slice kiwifruit on the batter in each well, then top with remaining batter.

Bake at 400 degrees F. for 20 minutes or until golden brown. Remove muffins to wire rack. While still warm, dust with sugar topping as follows: in a small jar shake the remaining 2 tablespoons sugar with a few drops red food coloring, then sprinkle a little colored sugar onto each muffin top.

Makes about 12 2½" muffins.

Each muffin contains about: 169 calories, 4g protein, 27g carbohydrate, 1g fiber, 5g fat, 46mg cholesterol, 116mg sodium.

September: Labor Day Then Back to School

As the summer heat eases and nights cool, the subtly-changing season brings a different pace in the kitchen; on the first Monday of September, Labor Day is summer's last fling.

Nowadays the original meaning of Labor Day, the annual celebration of the pride and dignity of American workers is sometimes overlooked. The holiday was originally a demonstration of the militancy of the Labor movement, when the first showing was held in New York City in 1882, promoted by an Irish-American labor leader, Peter McGuire, a carpenter by trade. But why in September? McGuire said "It would come at the most pleasant season of the year, nearly midway between the Fourth of July and Thanksgiving, to fill a wide gap in the chronology of legal holidays."

On September 5, 1882, about 10,000 workers left work and marched from Union Square up Fifth Avenue to 42nd Street in the morning, followed by speeches, picnics and dancing in the afternoon, and a fireworks display that evening. The holiday soon became a regular feature of the American calendar, and has since evolved into a whole weekend marking the end of the long vacation and the beginning of school.

The start of school coincides with the fresh apples of the fall season, when the crisp, colorful fruit come in abundance. English colonists planted orchards as early as 1625, making apples the mainstay of cooking in those days. The fruit was particularly favored because it could be pressed into cider, the American drink of choice in colonial times. Small wonder that villages in New England still have charming old cider mills with wooden presses crushing the fruit and scenting the air.

An apple for the teacher? Not nowadays, although the custom possibly started in early days when hard-working teachers in public schools were not always salaried, and in rural communities they were given local produce instead, as a legitimate way of paying them and showing appreciation. Another explanation may be that students offered them when they wanted to curry favor and ensure good grades!

Spiced Apple Muffins

These muffins will bring to mind the spicy fragrance of warm home-made apple pie. Mm! Laced with apples and apple cider, they are perfect for offering to guests during the Labor Weekend; and for school days, slip them into lunch bags or enjoy them after class with a tall glass of milk. The freshman can take them packed in a box to the college dorm as comfort food to share with friends. The apple gives the muffins moistness and great keeping qualities—but they won't stay around for long!

1 small apple (Gala variety), raw, unpeeled
2 cups unbleached all-purpose flour
1 teaspoon baking powder
½ teaspoon baking soda
¾ teaspoon salt
½ teaspoon ground cinnamon
¼ teaspoon ground cloves
½ cup light brown sugar, lightly packed
1 large egg
1 cup apple cider
¼ cup vegetable oil
½ cup coarsely chopped walnuts

Position rack in center of oven, preheat oven to 400 degrees F. and coat muffin wells with nonstick cooking spray. On a chopping board, core and finely dice apple, then set aside.

In a 2½ quart mixing bowl sift flour, baking powder, baking soda, salt, cinnamon and cloves. Add brown sugar and stir lightly to blend, making a well in center.

In a 1½ quart bowl whisk egg, cider and oil. Beat thoroughly, and add to flour mixture, stirring only until flour is moistened. Add walnuts and chopped apple. Spoon into prepared muffin wells.

Bake at 400 degrees F. for 20 to 25 minutes. Leave in pan for 5 minutes, then turn onto wire rack to cool slightly. Serve with apple butter if desired (see page 182).

Makes about 12 2½" muffins.

Each muffin (without apple butter spread) contains about: 206 calories, 3.5g protein, 30g carbohydrate, 1g fiber, 8g fat, 18mg cholesterol, 204mg sodium.

October: Halloween

It's time for witches, bats and black cats, ghosts and goblins, and big orange pumpkins carved into Jack o' Lanterns. Where did it all begin?

American-style Halloween is really a mixture of Druid practices from the Celts of northern and western Europe, Devil worship and other pagan and Christian religious beliefs brought over by Gaelic immigrants. Samhain had been an ancient Celtic New Year's pagan festival celebrated on November 1 until medieval churchmen re-named it All Hallow's Day to honor departed Christian saints.

Back in the ninth century it was believed that October 31 (the night before All Hallows Day) was the night of the year when unsettled bad spirits were most likely to visit. Masked and costumed villagers would band together to ward off the dreaded ghosts and witches said to swarm down from "places beyond." They would set large bonfires around the village, and to protect their houses they made rustic lamps by hollowing out the centers of large rutabagas, turnips and potatoes, carving faces on the surface and setting candles inside. When the Irish reached the United States, they continued the custom by using large American field pumpkins and winter squashes for the spooky flickering Jack o' Lanterns.

Centuries later, traditions evolved to an evening of general mischief: young men would roam the countryside, pulling practical jokes, many of which were destructive. Buildings were torn down or burned; livestock slaughtered or chased away.

Even now the traditions are continuing to evolve so that the neighborhood custom of "trick or treating" for candies is on the wane, and the current emphasis is more on costume parties and contests, and spookily decorated houses. One enduring motif of the evening is the pumpkin, decorating porches and doorways, festive buffets and dining-room centerpieces.

Pumpkin Currant Loaf

This spicy quick-bread is best baked the day before you need it. It's perfect for Halloween parties.

2 cups unbleached all-purpose flour
2 teaspoons baking powder
1 teaspoon *each* salt and ground cinnamon
½ teaspoon *each* baking soda and ground nutmeg
1 cup canned cooked pumpkin purée
¾ cup granulated sugar
½ cup nonfat skim milk
1 large egg
¼ cup (½ stick) melted butter or soy margarine
½ cup *each* chopped pecans and dried Zante currants
Pumpkin Spread (see Chapter 6, page 194)

Position rack in center of oven, preheat oven to 350 degrees F., and lightly grease a 9 x 5 x 3" loaf pan.

In a 2½ quart bowl sift the first six ingredients together; stir to blend and make a well in center.

In a 1½ quart bowl combine pumpkin, sugar, milk, egg and melted butter. Beat thoroughly, then add to flour mixture. Stir only until blended. Gently fold in pecans and currants. Spread in prepared loaf pan.

Bake at 350 degrees F. for 60 to 70 minutes, or until cake tester or toothpick inserted in center comes out clean. Leave in pan for 10 minutes, then turn out onto wire rack to cool. Serve sliced with Pumpkin Spread.

Makes one 9 x 5 x 3" loaf, about 14 slices.

Each slice (without Pumpkin Spread) contains about: 191 calories, 3g protein, 31g carbohydrate, 1.5g fiber, 6.5g fat, 24mg cholesterol, 273mg sodium.

November: Thanksgiving

Thanksgiving on the last Thursday in November is essentially a day of feasting—and an especially American feast—a time for celebrating with family and close friends, the major cooking day of the year. Many people worship together in the morning, to give thanks for their prosperity, followed by a meal of bountiful proportions later in the day. It can also be a day for sharing with the less fortunate, providing a holiday meal for the homeless or those who don't fit the Norman Rockwell image, so that no one goes hungry.

Since ancient times, people have had a feast at the end of the growing season, after the last crops were gathered, harvested and safely stored. So when the Pilgrim Fathers settled in New England nearly 400 years ago, they gave thanks in celebration of the first abundant harvest—a feast lasting for three days. Wampanoag Indians helped the Pilgrims celebrate by bringing their own foods, presenting a table spread with venison, gamebirds, oysters, eels, seafood, leeks and a variety of greens, wild plums and dried berries. A rich tradition was firmly established in the new land.

In the early days of the settlers, Thanksgiving dinner was probably the last big meal of the season when food was plentiful, before the frugality of the harsh winter months. It became a national holiday when Abraham Lincoln declared it so in 1863, after Sarah Josepha Hale, editor of *Godey's Lady's Book*, had urged that a day be set aside "to offer to God our tribute of joy and gratitude for the blessings of the year."

Cranberries must always have been a feature of the Thanksgiving feast; long before Europeans arrived, they were an important wild fruit for Native Americans, who ate them raw in spite of the fruit's natural sharpness. When they cooked the berries, they sweetened them with maple sugar or wild honey, or pounded them with dried meat and melted animal fat to make a northeast version of pemmican. New England sea captains valued cranberries for their crew on long ocean voyages, as a preventive against scurvy, when they were unable to obtain citrus fruits.

Cranberry Orange Bread

America is the only country that cultivates cranberries in any quantity. Harvesting begins in late September, and berries can be purchased in markets from October through January. Because they freeze well, right in the bag from the market, they can be bought, stored, and used all year.

This loaf studded with tart ruby cranberries and sparked with fresh orange juice makes a splendid contribution to the Thanksgiving table. It will slice better without being crumbly if baked the preceding day.

1 cup cranberries, fresh or frozen thawed
1⅞ cups unbleached all-purpose flour
1½ teaspoons baking powder
½ teaspoon baking soda
1 teaspoon salt
1 teaspoon dried granulated orange peel
⅞ cup granulated sugar
1 large egg
¼ cup (½ stick) melted butter or soy margarine
¾ cup freshly squeezed orange juice
½ cup chopped walnuts

Position rack in center of oven, preheat oven to 350 degrees F. and grease a 9 x 5 x 3" loaf pan. Wash cranberries in a colander and blot dry with paper towel. Chop berries coarsely in a food chopper then set aside.

In a 2½ quart bowl sift flour, baking powder, baking soda, salt, dried orange peel and sugar; stir to blend and make a well in center.

In a 1½ quart bowl whisk egg, melted butter and orange juice. Add to dry ingredients, mixing just enough to moisten. Fold in cranberries and nuts. Spoon into prepared loaf pan.

Bake at 350 degrees F. for about 1 hour, or until a test toothpick inserted in center comes out clean. Allow loaf to remain in pan 10 minutes before turning out onto wire rack to cool. Serve in neat slices.

Makes one 9 x 5 x 3" loaf, about 14 slices.

Each slice contains about: 181 calories, 3g protein, 28g carbohydrate, 1g fiber, 6.5g fat, 24mg cholesterol, 256mg sodium.

December:
The Christmas Season

The symbols of Christmas abound: carols, candles and greetings cards, Christmas trees, church bells and sleigh bells, manger scenes and mistletoe, holly and hanging up stockings, parades and poinsettias, twinkling lights and starry-eyed children.

St. Nicholas was the traditional bringer of gifts to Dutch children on his feast day, December 6, but when the holiday came to America, Sinterklaas became Santa Claus and the date moved to the 25th.

The custom of exchanging gifts is often linked to the visit of the Wise Men to Bethlehem when they brought gifts of gold, frankincense and myrrh to the Christ Child.

Red and green are the dominant colors for Christmas, reflecting the ancient use of berried-holly boughs when Romans festooned windows during their Saturnalia, as an offering to the spirits of the dark forests surrounding villages.

The Christmas tree has its origins in Europe where people held the pagan belief that evergreen trees were powerful beings of the Spirit World. By the sixteenth century, German families were cutting pine and fir trees to bring into their homes and calling them "Christ trees," to be decorated with fruit, cookies and candies, and to light them with candles during the holiday season. When, in the nineteenth century, Prince Albert of Saxe-Coburg married Queen Victoria, he brought the German custom of the *Christ baum* to England where it became popular; German immigrants brought the idea of decorated trees to the United States, although it was several decades before the custom was universal.

Until the eighteenth century in England, the traditional Christmas cup of cheer was *wassail*: a mixture of ale, roasted apples, sugar and spices, and occasionally eggs or cream, served hot from giant "wassail bowls." Gradually the brew was replaced by the nineteenth-century invention of eggnogs: those rich velvety blends of eggs, cream and spices laced with liquor.

Eggnog Muffins

Commercial versions of dairy eggnog are available during the holiday season from supermarkets. Light eggnog contains significantly less fat and therefore fewer calories, and it is this product that makes a rich-tasting muffin for the holidays, decked out in red and green. In the true spirit of Christmas, a package of these home-made muffins makes a welcome gift for a friend or neighbor.

1⅞ cups unbleached all-purpose flour
3 teaspoons baking powder
½ teaspoon *each* salt and ground nutmeg
1 large egg
1 cup commercial *light* eggnog
¼ cup (½ stick) melted butter or soy margarine
¼ cup *each* red and green glacé cherries

Line muffin wells with holly-patterned paper cases.

In a 2½ quart mixing bowl sift flour, baking powder, salt and nutmeg. Stir to blend and make a well in center.

In a 1½ quart bowl whisk egg, eggnog and melted butter; beat thoroughly. Add all at once to the flour mixture, stirring just until flour is moistened. Toss in glacé cherries and stir lightly. Spoon into prepared muffin wells.

Bake in a preheated oven at 400 degrees F. for 20 to 25 minutes.

Makes about 12 2½" muffins.

Each muffin contains about: 157 calories, 3.5g protein, 24g carbohydrate, 1g fiber, 5g fat, 36mg cholesterol, 228mg sodium.

Chapter 4

Sweet and Easy

The calendar indicates the traditional and official holidays each year, but unofficially there are countless more: the traditions we create within the family circle and among friends—birthdays, anniversaries, confirmations, as well as other great times that help us through dull uneventful days—those little occasions to be celebrated in style, with all the fare, flare and finery we can muster, and all the care and warmth that make such moments more memorable. Or maybe you simply want to brighten up the winter, welcome the spring and celebrate autumn. Or create a family fiesta, have a beach-party, welcome a new neighbor or have a neighborhood pot-luck.

Whatever the occasion, whether you're planning an elegant stylish commemorative dinner, a home-style supper, or wanting to fill a box with something special to mail to a sick friend as a thoughtful gesture, the wholesome goodness of these muffins will help make the event distinctive and special. They have great taste and good nutrition in every bite, and are not too sweet. The muffins are simple to make and simply delicious—and sometimes the simplest ideas outlast all the rest when they come from the heart.

Springtime Snow in California

The almond tree in bloom is strikingly beautiful. Almond country in the United States is the San Joaquin Valley in California, where from mid-February to mid-March, the orchards bear the frothy pure white or delicate pink blooms, and petals fall like snow upon the ground—although the area where almond trees flourish rarely sees real snow. Springtime can dazzle your senses: a panorama of blossoms, sweet fragrances wafted by a light breeze, and the air filled with the buzz of honey bees as they pollinate the orchards and groves.

Almonds were probably natives of Asia Minor, and even before historic times they were cultivated in countries of the Eastern Mediterranean and the Middle East. Archeologists have found fossil remains of the nuts at the Neolithic level under the palace of Knossos in Crete; the Romans called it the "Greek nut." The Egyptians valued almonds as a fine oil in cosmetics—and even today almond oil is the basis for hand creams and face lotions.

In the Near East, where people cultivated almond trees and sugar cane for thousands of years, they developed the popular confection marzipan, a delicate paste of ground almonds and sugar. The Persians knew it as early as A.D. 965, and later the Crusaders brought it to countries of Western Europe, particularly Germany.

Almonds are of two types—bitter and sweet: since the bitter ones are generally cheaper, they are used to make cooking oil and flavoring extracts for food and liqueurs. The more familiar sweet almonds are for eating whole and for cooking.

To blanch shelled almonds, cover with boiling water in a small bowl, let stand 2 minutes, then drain. Cover with cold water and rub off skins with the fingers. Blot dry on paper towel.

Almond Coffee Cake

A delicious quick-bread that you'll enjoy serving for weekend breakfast or brunch for a few friends. With crunchy almonds as topping, and tender crumb below, it's irresistible!

1⅞ cups unbleached all-purpose flour
3 teaspoons baking powder
½ teaspoon salt
⅓ cup granulated sugar
1 large egg
1 cup nonfat skim milk
¼ cup (½ stick) melted butter or soy margarine
1 teaspoon almond extract
½ cup golden raisins
½ teaspoon ground allspice
2 tablespoons cold butter
⅓ cup light brown sugar
⅓ cup chopped blanched almonds

Lightly grease an 8" square baking pan.

Sift first four ingredients in a 2½ quart mixing bowl, stir to blend and make a well in center.

In a 1½ pint mixing bowl whisk egg, milk, melted butter and almond extract, then add all at once to flour mixture. Stir only until flour is moistened. Gently fold in raisins, then pour into prepared baking pan. Lightly dust batter with allspice.

Prepare topping: in a 1½ pint bowl cut butter into fine pieces, add brown sugar and nuts. Sprinkle evenly on top of batter.

Bake in a preheated oven at 400 degrees F. for about 25 to 30 minutes, or until a toothpick inserted in center comes out clean. Place pan on a wire rack for about 10 minutes to cool slightly (unless you can't wait!). Cut into squares while still warm.

Makes 16 2" squares.

Each square contains about: 167 calories, 3g protein, 25g carbohydrate, 1g fiber, 6g fat, 25mg cholesterol, 187mg sodium.

Spice Up Your Life

Sweet spices can do more than flavor baked goods and desserts; they enliven and enhance soups, salad dressings and vegetables, and give a welcome lift to otherwise bland foods. Try these combinations:

Allspice

Pea soup, minestrone, cottage cheese, French dressing, eggplant, sweet potatoes, mincemeat and fruit pies.

Caraway seed

Potato soup, vegetable soup, cole slaw, potato salad, cabbage, cauliflower, sauerkraut, stuffings, rye bread, spice cake, cornbread.

Cardamom seed

Green pea soup, fruit salads, rice, baked beans, cakes, cookies and gingerbread.

Cinnamon

Fruit soup, Waldorf salad, fruit salad, sweet potatoes, broiled bananas, barbecue sauce, cakes, cookies, puddings, pies and breads.

Cloves

Tomato soup, mixed fruit salads, sweet potatoes, rice, tomatoes, cakes, cookies, pies and puddings.

Ginger

Bean soup, mixed fruit salads, beets, carrots, squash, gingerbread, cakes and cookies.

Nutmeg, Mace

Mushroom soup, spinach soup, mixed fruit salad, glazed carrots, cauliflower, spinach, ice cream, cakes, cookies and puddings.

Saffron

Vegetable soup, rice salads, rice casseroles, fruit breads, saffron buns and dumplings.

Sesame seed

Tossed green salads, asparagus, tomatoes, cakes, cookies, biscuits, breads and pastry.

Turmeric

Creamed soups, chowders, curries, rice and sauces.

(for Herb ideas, please see page 156)

Apricot Walnut Loaf

Golden brown, flecked with tart pieces of apricot, and crunchy nuts, this handsome loaf makes a delicious dessert with a fragrant cup of herbal tea.

½ cup chopped dried California apricots
1½ cups unbleached all-purpose flour
3 teaspoons baking powder
½ teaspoon *each* salt and ground nutmeg
¼ teaspoon baking soda
¼ cup unprocessed wheat bran
½ cup granulated sugar
1 tablespoon grated orange peel
1 large egg
¾ cup nonfat skim milk
¼ cup (½ stick) melted butter or soy margarine
½ cup chopped walnuts
Orange glaze (optional, see below)

Position rack in center of oven, preheat oven to 350 degrees F. and lightly grease a 9 x 5 x 3" loaf pan.

Snip dried apricots with kitchen scissors dipped in hot water; set aside.

In a 2½ quart bowl sift flour, baking powder, salt, nutmeg and baking soda. Stir in bran, sugar and orange peel, blend together and make a well in center.

In a 1½ pint bowl whisk egg, milk and melted butter. Add to flour mixture, stirring only until flour is moistened. Gently fold in walnuts. Don't overbeat. Spoon into prepared loaf pan.

Bake at 350 degrees F. for about 1 hour, or until a toothpick inserted in center comes out clean. Cool 10 minutes before removing from pan and turning onto a wire rack.

Optional glaze: in a small bowl mix ½ cup confectioners' sugar and 2 tablespoons undiluted concentrated orange juice until smooth (makes ¼ cup glaze). When completely cool, drizzle glaze over top and sides.

Makes one 9 x 5 x 3" loaf, about 14 slices.

Each slice (without glaze) contains about: 166 calories, 3.5g protein, 25g carbohydrate, 1.5g fiber, 6.5g fat, 24mg cholesterol, 207mg sodium.

Bananas with Appeal

The thick leathery leaves rustle gently in the warm breeze, sheltering the big bunches of ripening bananas gracefully bending towards the ground. A tropical atmosphere. Where are we? Panama or Ecuador, perhaps? Sunny Honduras or a Caribbean island? Think again.

This is California's first commercial banana garden, with the "trees" growing on a narrow shelf of land protected by 300 foot high bluffs along the coast at La Conchita (Ventura County), with weather tempered by the Pacific Ocean.

Think you know what a banana should *look* like? Yellow, slightly curved finger-shaped, about 5 or 6 inches long. But if you have traveled to banana-growing countries, you probably know that bananas grow in hundreds of sizes, shapes and colors—some red, salmon pink or a soft gold-red.

Think you know what a banana should *taste* like? Supermarket varieties are often pleasant but so mild as to be rather bland. At La Conchita the bananas are organically grown and allowed to mature longer on the plants; the cooler climate and special growing conditions result in fruit with more sweetness and concentrated flavor, and sometimes intensely perfumed.

The frond-shaded *palapa* (fruit-stand) offers freshly-picked "hands" of seldom-seen varieties—not only the sweet dessert types but also the starchier vegetable-like kinds for sautéing or baking. The standard grocery store variety is usually the Grand Nain or the Valery; here you can try Manzano, Blue Java, Brazilian (or Ladyfinger), Cardaba or Iholena and many more, including the Ae Ae, the banana originally eaten only by Hawaiian royalty.

Did you know that bananas don't grow on trees? Botanists classify them as an herb because the plant has no wood: the thick stalk is composed of leaves wrapped together tightly. Tallest herbs in the world, bananas grow up to 25 feet high with leaves two feet long. They originated in Southeast Asia on the Malay Peninsula about a million years ago, but many Americans saw and tasted the fruit for the first time in 1876 when they were displayed at the Philadelphia Exposition along with other new wonders of the world!

Banana Marmalade Loaf

For easy slicing without crumbling, make the loaf the day before serving. After cooling, wrap well.

3 ripe bananas
2 large eggs, beaten until light
⅓ cup vegetable oil
½ cup orange marmalade
1 cup unbleached all-purpose flour
½ cup whole-wheat flour
1 teaspoon baking soda
½ teaspoon salt
½ cup unprocessed wheat bran
⅔ cup light brown sugar
⅔ cup chopped walnuts

Position rack in center of oven, preheat oven to 350 degrees F., and lightly grease a 9 x 5 x 3" loaf pan.

In a 1½ quart bowl, mash bananas with a fork and beat until smooth. Whisk in eggs, oil and marmalade. Set aside.

In a 2½ quart bowl sift flours, baking soda and salt. Stir in bran and sugar to blend, and make a well in center. Add banana mixture to flour mixture and stir until flour is moistened. Gently fold in nuts. Spread in prepared loaf pan.

Bake at 350 degrees F. for about 45 minutes to 1 hour. To prevent overbrowning, cover loaf lightly with a tent of aluminum foil for the last 10 minutes. Check doneness with a toothpick inserted in center. Cool in pan 10 minutes before turning out onto a wire rack.

Makes one 9 x 5 x 3" loaf, about 16 slices.

Each slice contains about: 206 calories, 3.5g protein, 32g carbohydrate, 2g fiber, 8.5g fat, 26mg cholesterol, 132mg sodium.

Edwards Mansion: Nostalgia for a Proud Victorian

The old house still stands among orange trees—a delightful reminder of a bygone and gracious era in California's orange-growing history, when the small settlement of Redlands was described as the "Navel Orange Capital of the World."

Back in 1890, pioneer citizen and citrus grower James S. Edwards planned to build a magnificent fourteen-room house for his family in Redlands. The original salmon-pink building took over a year to construct; people marvelled at the great care being taken over the detail of gables, bay windows and ornate doorways, and the finish of the handsome flight of stairs to the sunny terrace. The house became a prominent landmark on Cajon Street, situated on twenty acres on a slight rise of ground from which you could see in all directions over the young orange trees.

When Mr. Edwards took up residence, hired a Chinese cook to prepare meals for the family and Chinese workers to tend the orange trees, the great Victorian masterpiece became home to the Edwards family for fifty years.

But during the 1960s the old home stood sadly unused. It served as offices for a few years until developers bought the place in 1973, recognizing the house as a classic example of Victorian times. For the sum of one dollar, they purchased the old home which then suffered the indignity of being sliced into two sections and moved five miles to the western outskirts of Redlands, "with nary a window cracked," and then put together again. In its new location on Orange Tree Lane set among California's oldest fertile and picturesque orange groves, the house was beautifully refurbished and restored.

Private elegant luncheons and candlelit dinners are now served in the panelled antique-furnished rooms, at tables set with lace tablecloths and shining silverware. The tiny wedding chapel nearby provides a charming setting to recite marriage vows; as couples step outside, the confetti tossed to the newlyweds falls to the ground to blend with the delicate white petals wafted from the fragrant trees.

California Orange Muffins

When Edwards Mansion was run as a restaurant, the menu featured orange muffins warm from the ovens in the mansion kitchen. This recipe for California Orange Muffins has been updated to recapture the appeal and fresh taste of tree-ripened fruit.

1½ cups unbleached all-purpose flour
¼ cup granulated sugar
1 teaspoon baking powder
¼ teaspoon *each* salt and baking soda
1 teaspoon grated orange peel
1 large egg
¼ cup nonfat skim milk
¼ cup fresh orange juice
⅓ cup melted butter or soy margarine
½ cup diced orange sections

Position rack in center of oven, preheat oven to 400 degrees F. and line muffin wells with paper cases.

In a 2½ quart mixing bowl sift flour, sugar, baking powder, salt and baking soda; add orange peel, stir to blend and make a well in center.

In a 1½ quart bowl whisk egg, milk, orange juice and butter. Beat thoroughly, then add all at once to flour mixture. Stir just until blended and flour is moistened. Add orange dice. Spoon batter into prepared muffin wells until two-thirds full.

Bake at 400 degrees F. for about 25 minutes or until a test toothpick inserted in centers comes out clean.

Makes about 12 2½" muffins.

Each muffin contains about: 132 calories, 2.5g protein, 18g carbohydrate, 1g fiber, 6g fat, 31mg cholesterol, 149mg sodium.

A Glossary for Chocolate Lovers (Part 1)

Baker's Chocolate: A registered trademark of Kraft General Foods, Inc.; may be semi-sweet.

Baking (bitter) chocolate: Chocolate liquor that has been cooled and molded into blocks or 1-oz squares. Unsweetened cooking chocolate. A concentrated source of caffeine: 1 oz has about 26 mg (compared to 60 mg in a cup of coffee).

Cacao beans: From pods of the cacao tree, *Theobroma cacao* (from Greek, "food of the gods"), growing in tropics, 20 degrees north and south of the Equator, mainly in West Africa and Brazil. Harvested mostly from May to December.

Carob: An edible pod of a Mediterranean tree, *Ceratonia siliqua*, unrelated to cacao, but from which comes a product, "St. John's Bread," resembling chocolate. Carob, sold in health-food stores as whole seeds, unsweetened chips or toasted powder, is naturally sweet (46% natural sugars), caffeine-free, and considered more nutritious than chocolate.

Chocolate chips: Usually semi-sweet, with about 40% sugar, 60% bitter chocolate. Regular and miniature sizes.

Chocolate flavored: A product containing cocoa and/or chocolate liquor but insufficient to legally be called chocolate.

Chocolate drinks: Powder that may be pre-sweetened with sugar or artificial sweetener. In the U.S., the beverage is made with water; in France the base is milk. In Vienna, it's topped with mountains of real whipped cream; in America, with melted marshmallows and cinnamon sticks. In Brazil and Russia, they add coffee; in Mexico, they add cinnamon, almonds, orange peel, Sherry or coffee liqueur.

Chocolate liquor: Ground up "nibs" suspended in cocoa butter. The grinding process generates sufficient heat to liquify the cocoa butter. Not to be confused with a liqueur, chocolate liquor has no alcoholic content.

Chocolate milk: Milk that has been flavored with chocolate and sweetened with sugar, found in the dairy case.

Chocolate syrup: A combination of chocolate liquor or cocoa, sugar, water, salt and sometimes vanilla flavoring.

(Part 2 is on page 86)

Chocolate Doubles

Moist and rich-flavored, with both cocoa and chocolate chips to satisfy chocolate cravings, these muffins are surprisingly low in cholesterol.

1½ cups unbleached all-purpose flour
½ cup granulated sugar
¼ cup unsweetened cocoa powder
1 teaspoon baking soda
½ teaspoon salt
½ cup apple juice
¼ cup water
¼ cup (½ stick) melted butter or soy margarine
1 tablespoon mild vinegar
1 teaspoon vanilla extract
½ cup semi-sweet chocolate chips

Position rack in center of oven, preheat oven to 375 degrees F., and coat muffin wells with nonstick cooking spray.

In a 2½ quart mixing bowl sift flour, sugar, cocoa, baking soda and salt. Mix thoroughly to blend, and make a well in center.

In a 1½ quart bowl whisk apple juice, water, butter, vinegar and vanilla extract. Pour all at once into flour mixture and stir just until flour is moistened. Do not overmix. Gently fold in chocolate chips. Spoon into prepared muffin wells.

Bake at 375 degrees F. for about 20 to 25 minutes, or until a test toothpick inserted in centers comes out clean. Remove from pan and cool on a wire rack.

Makes about 12 2½" muffins.

Each muffin contains about: 168 calories, 2g protein, 26g carbohydrate, 1g fiber, 7g fat, 10mg cholesterol, 211mg sodium.

A Glossary for Chocolate Lovers (Part 2)

Cocoa butter: A vegetable fat extracted from chocolate liquor.

Cocoa powder: The dry solids that remain after cocoa butter has been extracted from chocolate liquor.

Dark sweet chocolate: A mixture of at least 15% chocolate liquor with added cocoa butter and sugar. It has a higher proportion of sugar than semi-sweet chocolate.

Dutch process cocoa: Darker color and mild mellow flavor compared to regular cocoa powder. "Dutching" means processing nibs or chocolate liquor with potassium carbonate to neutralize the natural acids.

German's sweet chocolate: Not from Germany, but invented by a Mr. German; a proprietary name of the Baker Chocolate Company (Kraft General Foods, Inc.).

Instant cocoa mix: A combination of cocoa butter and sugar, with lecithin to separate granules to make a smooth drink. The mixture may contain 70% sugar.

Milk chocolate: A mixture of at least 10% chocolate liquor with added cocoa butter, sugar and milk or cream.

Nibs: The kernels of the cacao beans. After cleaning and roasting the beans to bring out flavor and aroma, the outer shells are removed, leaving the "meaty" nibs.

Pre-melted baking chocolate: Unsweetened cocoa mixed with vegetable oil, sold in foil or plastic envelopes ready for baking.

Semi-sweet chocolate: A combination of chocolate liquor, added cocoa butter and sugar. Must contain at least 35% chocolate liquor. Often sold in the form of chocolate chips.

Synthetic or artificial chocolate: Imitation products resembling chocolate but containing no cocoa beans. Ingredients vary and may also include synthetic milk and artificial sweetener.

White chocolate: A combination of vegetable fat (cocoa butter), milk solids and sugar, but no cocoa solids. In other words, chocolate without chocolate! Available in white, dark or pastel colors. White chocolate should not be substituted for chocolate in recipes, unless specified.

(Part 1 is on page 84)

Choco-Mayo Muffins

Easy to make, quick to bake, keep this recipe handy for when you don't happen to have eggs in the house, time is short, and you want to offer "something chocolate" to guests.

2 cups unbleached all-purpose flour
4 tablespoons unsweetened cocoa powder
1 cup granulated sugar
2 teaspoons baking powder
1 teaspoon baking soda
½ teaspoon salt
1 cup commercial mayonnaise
1 cup water
1 teaspoon vanilla extract

Position rack in center of oven, preheat oven to 375 degrees F., and coat muffin wells with nonstick cooking spray.

In a 2½ quart mixing bowl sift the first six ingredients, stir to mix thoroughly and make a well in center.

In a 1½ quart bowl whisk mayonnaise with water and vanilla until well blended and smooth. Add all at once to flour mixture and stir just until flour is moistened. Spoon into prepared muffin wells.

Bake at 375 degrees F. for 20 to 25 minutes, until a test toothpick inserted in centers comes out clean. Cool in pan 5 minutes before removing to a wire rack.

Makes about 12 2½" muffins.

Each muffin contains about: 277 calories, 3g protein, 34g carbohydrate, 1g fiber, 15g fat, 11mg cholesterol, 330mg sodium.

Coconuts: Meat and Milk of the Tropics

In the hot humid tropics, coconut palms sway to the trade winds, giving important food to one-third of the world's population. A coconut palm growing in a tropical backyard has been likened to the family cow on farms in temperate zones, since much of the cuisine in diverse areas of southeast Asia and India is based on coco-water (the cool clear juice from immature coconuts), the white "meat" from the mature nuts, and coconut "milk" squeezed from the grated meat.

Although immature nuts are too perishable to ship, the ripened coconuts are generally available in U.S. markets year-round. The rough appearance of the hard outer shells may intimidate, but with a few tricks they are easily opened to offer pulp that is superior to the ready-bagged, flaked, pre-sweetened product.

How do you tackle a fresh coconut? Choose a large coconut without any cracks. It should sound full of liquid when you shake it. Pierce the "eyes" with an ice pick, skewer or screwdriver, then drain the liquid and reserve it for another use.

Bake the coconut in a 400 degree F. oven for 20 minutes. Tap it all over with a hammer to loosen the shell. Crack with a hammer, and remove flesh from the shell by levering it out carefully with the point of a strong knife. Peel away brown membrane with a vegetable peeler, and cut the coconut meat into small pieces. Feed the pieces into a blender in small batches, transfering it to a bowl as it is ground. Or grate the pieces on the fine side of a grater. A large coconut generally yields about 4 cups of meat.

To toast: spread the grated coconut meat in a thin layer in a shallow pan or baking sheet, and bake at 350 degrees F. for 10 to 15 minutes, until golden brown. Stir frequently during baking for even browning. Use toasted coconut in candy recipes, as a garnish for fruit salads or a topping for a simple cake. Refrigerate it in a tightly covered jar until ready to use.

Coconut Apricot Muffins

These muffins are delicious with a summer fruit salad, with a special cup of coffee as a dessert, or just anytime.

1¾ cups unbleached all-purpose flour
2 teaspoons baking powder
½ teaspoon salt
½ cup granulated sugar
1 large egg
1 cup nonfat skim milk
½ cup vegetable oil
1 teaspoon almond extract
1 cup flaked coconut, lightly toasted (see opposite page)
12 teaspoons apricot preserves

Line 12 muffin wells with paper cases.

In a 2½ quart mixing bowl sift flour, baking powder, salt and sugar; stir to blend and make a well in center.

In a 1½ pint mixing bowl whisk egg, milk, oil and almond extract. Add all at once to flour mixture and stir just until flour is moistened. Gently fold in coconut to distribute evenly. Spoon *half* the batter into prepared muffin wells. Drop a teaspoon of preserves into each well, then top with remaining batter.

Bake in a preheated oven at 400 degrees F. for about 20 minutes. Cool muffins about 5 minutes, then remove to a wire rack to cool.

Makes about 12 2½" muffins.

Each muffin contains about: 234 calories, 3.5g protein, 29g carbohydrate, 1g fiber, 12g fat, 18mg cholesterol, 162mg sodium.

A Good Cup of Java

There's nothing in the world like good coffee, whether shared with others or savored in a quiet moment alone, a beverage enjoyed by about one-third of the world's population.

Coffee appears to have originated in Ethiopia—the Horn of Africa. One story, whether truth or myth, dates back to A.D. 850 when an Abyssinian (Ethiopian) goatherd named Kaldi discovered his goats prancing excitedly around a group of shiny dark-leaved shrubs bearing red berries. After tasting the berries himself, Kaldi also began to dance, realizing what had prompted his herd's unusual behavior. Kaldi shared his discovery with monks at a nearby monastery: the monks boiled the bright berries and found the beverage helped them ward off drowsiness through long religious services.

Most species of the coffee plant grow wild in the tropics of the Eastern Hemisphere; the earliest known cultivated coffee was probably *Coffea arabica* from the Arabian peninsula. For centuries, Abyssinian tribesmen had *eaten* the coffee beans; it was the Arabs across the Red Sea who later turned the beans into a hot drink.

Orthodox priests suspected that the stimulating effect was intoxication and banned it by the Quran, but despite prohibition, coffee drinking spread rapidly among Arabs and their neighbors. In Turkey they took coffee drinking seriously: Turkish bridegrooms would have to promise in their marriage vows to always provide their wives with coffee; breaking the pledge was grounds for divorce.

Coffee was imported into Italy in 1580 through Venice, and during the 16th and 17th centuries, one European country after another took up the habit. Up to the end of the 17th century, supplies of coffee beans had come almost entirely from Yemen province in southern Arabia, controlled by astute traders through the port of Mocha (Al Mukha). But when demand outstripped supplies, the Arabic monopoly was broken by the Dutch who established new plantations on Java and other Indonesian islands in the 17th century. By the 20th century, when plant disease threatened coffee growing in older plantations, the largest production became centered in Brazil.

Coffee Bars

Richly flavored with coffee and hint of mocha, and crunchy with nuts, these bars make a good breakfast or a mid-morning snack.

1 cup unbleached all-purpose flour
2 tablespoons dry unsweetened cocoa powder
2 teaspoons baking powder
¼ teaspoon baking soda
¼ cup granulated sugar
¾ cup whole-wheat flour
2 large eggs
1 cup cold strong black coffee (or 2 tablespoons instant
    coffee granules in 1 cup water)
1 teaspoon vanilla extract
¼ cup vegetable cooking oil
1 teaspoon ground cinnamon
Streusel topping:
    2 oz. (½ stick) cold butter
    ⅓ cup light brown sugar, lightly packed
    ⅓ cup (2 oz) chopped walnuts

Lightly grease a 9" square baking pan.

In a 2½ quart mixing bowl sift first five ingredients, stir in whole-wheat flour to blend, and make a well in center.

In a 1½ quart bowl whisk eggs, cooled coffee, vanilla extract and cooking oil, and add to flour mixture. Stir only until flour is moistened. Spread in prepared pan and sprinkle with cinnamon. Make streusel topping: in a small bowl chop butter into fine pieces, and mix in brown sugar and walnuts. Sprinkle evenly over pan batter.

Bake in a preheated oven at 400 degrees F. for 30 to 35 minutes or until a toothpick inserted in center comes out clean. Cool slightly. Cut into bars.

Makes 16 bars 2" x 2".

Each bar contains about: 159 calories, 3g protein, 18g carbohydrate, 1g fiber, 9g fat, 34mg cholesterol, 95mg sodium.

Cranberries: A Sign of Autumn

The word "cranberry" is a contraction of crane berry, because the pale pink blossoms are said to resemble the head of a crane. Most cranberries are still harvested from low-lying bogs which are flooded; the bushes are raked, the loosened berries float to the top and are then gathered. Good cranberries should bounce, so each berry undergoes the "bounce test," run over a bounce board: the soft ones that don't bounce, end up in the reject bin; the bouncers go to market.

Canned ready-made cranberry jelly is a convenience, but making your own from fresh berries is simple and well worth the effort. Serve the tart-sweet jelly as a relish, a spread on English muffins, a cake-filling, or as an ingredient in the muffins on the opposite page. The ruby-red jelly makes a beautiful gift for friends at holiday time.

Spiced Cranberry Jelly

1 lb fresh cranberries
2 cups boiling water
2" cinnamon stick
20 whole cloves
5 allspice berries
2 cups granulated sugar
¼ teaspoon salt

Wash and drain cranberries. Pick over to check for stems or damaged fruit. Place berries in a large saucepan with the boiling water. Tie cinnamon, cloves and allspice in a small square of cheesecloth and add to berries. Boil 20 minutes. Remove spice bag, rub fruit through a sieve. Return to saucepan and cook 3 minutes. Add sugar and salt, and cook 2 more minutes. Pour into jelly glasses and seal.

Makes about 4 cups.

One tablespoon contains about: 28 calories, 0 protein, 7g carbohydrate, .3g fiber, 0 fat, 0 cholesterol, 9mg sodium.

Cranberry Almond Muffins

These muffins can take pride of place on a holiday buffet table. Serve with hot spiced punch or cranberry juice cocktail.

2 cups unbleached all-purpose flour
1 teaspoon *each* baking powder and baking soda
½ teaspoon salt
¼ cup *each* light brown sugar and granulated sugar
Whites of 2 large eggs
¼ cup (½ stick) melted butter or soy margarine
1 cup nonfat plain yogurt
2 tablespoons nonfat skim milk
1 cup spiced cranberry jelly (see opposite page)
1½ teaspoons almond extract

Position rack in center of oven, preheat oven to 400 degrees F., and coat muffin wells with nonstick cooking spray.

In a 2½ quart mixing bowl sift flour, baking powder, baking soda and salt. Stir in sugars to blend, and make a well in center.

In a 1½ quart bowl whisk egg whites until foamy, add melted butter, yogurt, milk, cranberry jelly and almond extract. Beat well. Add all at once to flour mixture and stir just until flour is moistened and blended. Spoon into prepared muffin wells.

Bake at 400 degrees F. for 25 minutes, or until a test toothpick inserted in centers comes out clean. Turn out onto a wire rack to cool.

Makes about 12 2½" muffins.

Each muffin contains about: 192 calories, 4g protein, 35g carbohydrate, 1g fiber, 4g fat, 11mg cholesterol, 257mg sodium.

The Romantic Date

The varietal names on packages of dates in the market immediately fire the imagination to conjure up romantic scenes of Arabian nights, deserts, elegant palms, cool oases, and the minarets of the Middle East: Deglet Noor ("date of light"), Medjools, Zahidis, Halawys and Khadrawys.

The word "date" originated from the Greek *daktulos* meaning "finger," the shape of the fruit; in medieval Europe dates were called "finger apples," and even today there is a fine delicate Arabic variety called Bride's Fingers.

Wild dates have flourished in arid regions as early as about 50,000 B.C. and were one of the first fruits to be cultivated, domesticated by Sumerians of ancient Babylon at least 5,000 years ago. Enjoying "its feet in water and its head in the fires of heaven," it grew along riverbanks and the network of irrigation canals in southern Mesopotamia. Dates have been considered a source of wealth since remotest antiquity, and fed to the poor as a staple food even cheaper than grain in that area. They were eaten either fresh and whole, just picked from the tree, or dried simply by burying them in the hot desert sand, then compressed into blocks—a convenient food for desert nomads. In winter, they chopped up dried dates and mixed them with a little barley, or ate them as candies by blending them with almonds, pistachio nuts and sesame oil.

The deserts of North Africa and Iran are still the centers for the world's date growing. About 1,000 varieties of date palms are known, and in the *suq* of the Moroccan city of Fez, for instance, you can choose from thirty kinds of dates.

The dates you are most likely to see in U.S. markets are the Deglet Noor, which makes up about 85 percent of the dates produced in California's Coachella Valley; it's firm-fleshed, semi-dry, a lustrous dark amber and perhaps more sweet than other varieties. Medjools, once reserved for royalty because of their exquisite flavor, can reach a remarkable size and are soft and creamy; Zahidis are reddish brown and firm; Halawys are golden brown, soft and very sweet; and Khadrawys have a slight greenish tinge, soft and rich.

Date Nut Bread

This quick-bread has an attractive dark color; the dates give a rich flavor that is not too sweet. The loaf is best made the day before you need it, to slice easily and allow the flavors to blend and mellow.

1½ cups boiling water
1½ cups chopped dates
½ cup granulated sugar
¼ cup vegetable oil
1 large egg, well beaten
1 tablespoon lemon juice
2 cups unbleached all-purpose flour
2 teaspoons baking soda
1 teaspoon baking powder
¼ teaspoon salt
½ cup chopped walnuts

Position rack in center of oven; preheat oven to 350 degrees F. Lightly grease a 9 x 5 x 3" loaf pan, line with waxed paper and grease the paper.

In a 1½ quart mixing bowl pour boiling water over dates; set aside to cool, then add sugar, oil, beaten egg and lemon juice.

In a 2½ quart bowl sift flour, baking soda, baking powder and salt. Stir to blend and make a well in center. Gently stir in date-egg mixture until flour is just moistened. Fold in walnuts to distribute evenly. Spoon into prepared loaf pan.

Bake at 350 degrees F. for 60 to 70 minutes, or until a test toothpick inserted in center comes out clean. Allow to cool on a wire rack for 10 to 15 minutes before removing from pan. When cool, wrap well.

Makes one 9 x 5 x 3" loaf, about 16 slices.

Each slice contains about: 186 calories, 3g protein, 31g carbohydrate, 2g fiber, 6g fat, 13mg cholesterol, 162mg sodium.

Señor Feijo's Exotic Fruit

The feijoa (pronounced fay-JO-a or fay-YO-a) was named after Don J. da Silva Feijo, a botanist and Director of the Natural History Museum in San Sebastian, Spain. The sharp taste of the fruit is aromatic, with a mild pineapple-like flavor, hence it's sometimes referred to as pineapple guava.

Originally found wild in the mountains of southern Brazil, Paraguay, Uruguay and northern Argentina, the cultivated fruit is now grown extensively in New Zealand, and this crop reaches U.S. markets in spring and early summer. The small California crop arrives in the fall, in supermarkets and local farmers' markets.

The shape is similar to an elongated egg, the slightly bumpy skin is a dull avocado green, enclosing a creamy flesh that is pleasantly gritty, like a pear. Don't attempt to eat the fruit until it is properly ripe, or it will be very sharp and maybe bitter. As soon as the fruit is ripe, store in the refrigerator. Eat the pulp raw as a delicious dessert or in fruit salads; or cook it to a purée for a lovely ice cream topping, a filling for sponge cakes and tarts, or an addition in puddings, jams and fruit chutneys. Plus, of course, the purée makes a superb muffin ingredient.

Feijoa Purée-Syrup

4 ripe feijoas (½ lb)
¼ cup granulated sugar
¼ cup water

Slice feijoas in half crosswise and scoop out flesh, pulp and seeds with a small spoon, avoiding the bitter skin and bright-green membranes.

In a small saucepan (not aluminum, to avoid a chemical reaction), bring sugar and water to a boil, add fruit and return to boiling. Stir constantly, and cook about 5 minutes or until fruit is softened. Remove from heat and allow to cool. Mash with a fork or purée in blender. Store purée until needed in the refrigerator for up to a week, or in the freezer for several months.

Makes approximately ⅓ cup purée.

Feijoa Fancies

Since the feijoa is somewhat pungent, just a moderate amount is needed to make an unusual luxurious addition to muffins, to elevate their social status and intrigue your guests.

1¾ cups unbleached all-purpose flour
2 teaspoons baking powder
¼ teaspoon *each* baking soda and salt
¼ cup granulated sugar
1 large egg
¼ cup (½ stick) melted butter or soy margarine
½ cup buttermilk
½ cup freshly squeezed orange juice
⅓ cup feijoa purée-syrup (see opposite page)
1 teaspoon *each* vanilla extract and grated orange peel

Position rack in center of oven, preheat oven to 400 degrees F., and coat muffin wells with nonstick cooking spray.

In a 2½ quart bowl sift flour, baking powder, baking soda, salt and sugar. Stir to blend and make a well in center.

In a 1½ quart bowl whisk egg until light and foamy, add melted butter, buttermilk, orange juice, feijoa purée, vanilla and orange peel. Add buttermilk mixture to flour mixture and stir just until flour is moistened. Spoon into prepared muffin wells.

Bake at 400 degrees F. for 25 minutes, or until a test toothpick inserted in centers comes out clean. Cool slightly in pan for 5 minutes before turning muffins onto a wire rack. Serve warm.

Makes about 12 2½" muffins.

Each muffin contains about: 159 calories, 3g protein, 27g carbohydrate, 1g fiber, 5g fat, 28mg cholesterol, 172mg sodium.

The World of Ginger

The slightly biting flavor of ginger gives a lift to the taste of breads, sauces, curries and pickles. A native of southeast Asia, ginger was taken by traders to the countries of the Mediterranean basin by the first century A.D. By the 11th century, it was popular in England and made into fermented beers, ales and wines.

Known in China since ancient times, there they like to peel the rhizomes (underground stems) and preserve them by boiling in a syrup. Jars of beautifully designed fine porcelain are filled with the preserved ginger and presented as gifts during the Chinese New Year celebrations.

Ginger is a popular spice in Scandinavia: on December 13 each year in Sweden, the people celebrate Saint Lucia, the saint honored for bringing light at the darkest time of year. Girls wear crowns of candles and white robes in church pageants, and on Saint Lucia Day traditionally offer trays of coffee and spicy ginger cookies to their parents at daybreak.

Gingerbread, one of the most famous of all German regional specialties, has been serious business in Nüremberg for at least 600 years. In the days when professional guildsmen were in sole charge of communal ovens, commercial gingerbread was baked by members of an exclusive guild known as *Lebküchler*, rather than by homemakers or ordinary bakers. The city of Nüremberg is still known as the "Gingerbread Capital of the World."

The most delightful of all traditional German Christmas confections are the gingerbread houses (*Lebküchenhäuschen*) also known as *Knusperhäuschen* (houses that can be nibbled and munched)—a charming tradition that German settlers brought to the United States. Walls, roof and foundation formed with hard baked dough are held together with a "mortar" of special sugar frosting; sugar icicles drip from roofs, and snow-like icing fills the crevices.

Don't attempt to make a house with the gingerbread recipes in this book. Your local bookshop or public library has craft books giving special recipes and "house plans."

For more about ginger, please turn to page 188.

Gingerbread Deluxe

Double ginger gives an exquisite depth of flavor for a simple but elegant dessert. Serve with chilled fruit such as sliced pears or peaches, and plain or whipped cream.

1½ cups unbleached all-purpose flour
1 teaspoon *each* baking soda and ground ginger
½ teaspoon salt
2 large eggs
½ cup molasses
½ cup dairy sour cream
½ cup light brown sugar
½ cup (1 stick) melted butter or soy margarine
½ cup chopped preserved stem ginger, drained

Position rack in center of oven, preheat oven to 350 degrees F., and lightly grease a shallow 8" square pan.

In a 2½ quart mixing bowl sift first four ingredients, stir to blend and make a well in center.

In a 1½ quart mixing bowl whisk eggs, then add molasses, sour cream, brown sugar and melted butter. Beat well. Add to flour mixture and stir just until flour is moistened. Gently fold in preserved ginger to distribute evenly, and pour at once into prepared pan.

Bake at 350 degrees F. for about 30 minutes, or until a test toothpick inserted in center comes out clean. Cool slightly for 10 minutes in pan before turning out onto a wire rack. Cut into squares.

Makes 16 2" squares.

Each square contains about: 183 calories, 2.5g protein, 26g carbohydrate, .5g fiber, 8g fat, 45mg cholesterol, 193mg sodium.

A Taste of Honey: A Buying Guide

Honey gives a wonderful chewy quality and rich brown color to baked goods; they retain a moist freshness and dry out less quickly.

You can buy several hundred types of honey in the United States, each with its unique flavor derived from the nectar gathered from various flowers by domesticated bees. When you shop for honey, you first notice the range of color varying from palest gold to dark, rich amber brown. In general the color indicates its flavor: the darker the honey, the stronger it will be. Clover and orange blossom honeys are pale and mild-tasting. Buckwheat and wildflower honeys are usually dark-colored and strong in flavor. Dark rich-tasting honeys are wonderful on whole-wheat breads, but would be too strong and overpowering in muffins and quick-breads.

Buy honey in 12 oz or 16 oz jars; when you find your favorite flavor, five-pound cans are a more economical buy. Note the difference between *creamed* honey and honey *butter*: creamed has been whipped or "spun" and comes in jars or cartons. Honey butter sold in the dairy case is a blend of honey and butter, so will contain a greater number of calories because of the fat content. At certain times during the year, some markets sell square boxes of honey still in the comb; cut honeycomb in jars of honey is available all year.

Honey is best stored in a cool, dry place, but not in the refrigerator where it will soon harden and form sugar crystals. When honey turns hard and sugary, it's not spoiled. To re-liquify and dissolve the sugar crystals, simply place the jar in a pan of hot (not boiling) water until liquid; or heat the honey in a microwave-safe container in the microwave on HIGH for two to three minutes, stirring now and then. Avoid overheating honey, to protect color and flavor. For easy clean-up, first coat the measuring cup or spoon with nonstick cooking spray or oil, or dip it in water.

For more about honey, please turn to page 102.

Honey Ginger Muffins

Warm from the oven, these ginger-flecked muffins go well with mugs of hot spiced apple juice when the first days of autumn have a cold nip in the air—perfect to come home to, after an afternoon of raking leaves off the lawn!

1¼ cups whole-wheat flour
1 cup unbleached all-purpose flour
3 teaspoons baking powder
½ teaspoon salt
1 large egg
1 cup nonfat skim milk
⅓ cup mild honey, slightly warmed
¼ cup (½ stick) melted butter or soy margarine
½ cup finely chopped crystallized ginger

Line muffin wells with paper cases.

In a 2½ quart mixing bowl sift flours, baking powder and salt. Stir to blend and make a well in center.

In a 1½ quart bowl whisk egg, milk, honey and butter. Beat thoroughly. Stir all at once into flour mixture until just combined. Gently fold in crystallized ginger to distribute evenly. Spoon into prepared muffin wells.

Bake in preheated oven at 400 degrees F. for 20 to 25 minutes. Cool 5 minutes in pan then turn out onto a wire rack.

Makes about 12 2½" muffins.

Each muffin contains about: 182 calories, 4g protein, 32g carbohydrate, 2g fiber, 5g fat, 28mg cholesterol, 228mg sodium.

Honey in History

One of the oldest sweeteners known to humans must have been honey gathered from wild bees' nests and later from "domesticated" bees in the manmade structures we call hives. Early hives were made of clay, then later straw or wicker "skeps," and now of wood with frames upon which the bees build their natural comb.

Ancient peoples held honey in high esteem, giving it as a worthy offering to the gods and using it in funeral ceremonies, largely because they thought honey had mysterious and therefore magical origins: early Egyptians believed honey came from the tears of the sun god Ra; they used it for embalming, and a pharaoh's tomb wasn't complete unless it contained a sealed honey jar decorated with bee motifs. Virgil, the Roman poet, writes of "Heaven's gift, the honey from the skies;" Pliny speculated that "honey comes out of the air—at early dawn the leaves of trees are found bedewed with honey."

Honey was valued for its healing benefits: mildly antiseptic, it was used to treat burns and cuts, and in ancient Greece, Hippocrates recommended mixing honey with pepper and vinegar to treat feminine disorders. Fermented honey and water was made into mead, also called metheglin (from the Welsh *meddyglyn*, "physician") referring to the medicinal power of the alcoholic wine.

Although the Aztec emperor Montezuma once received seven hundred large jars of honey in tribute from conquered villagers, the honey must have come from exclusively-tropical bees native to the New World. Early peoples of North America weren't familiar with *Apis mellifera* until it was introduced about 1625 by settlers bringing colonies of European honey bees with them from Europe. With the advance of homesteading across the American West, these European bees swarmed into the trees across the land. Indians were surprised to discover that these wild nests contained a food of great sweetness that they ate with "greedy relish" when they tasted this superior honey for the first time.

Honey Raisin Bread

Moist and aromatic with honey. Bake this quick-bread the day before you intend to serve it to allow flavors to mellow.

2½ cups unbleached all-purpose flour
1 teaspoon baking powder
½ teaspoon *each* baking soda and salt
1 large egg
2 tablespoons melted butter or soy margarine
½ cup honey, slightly warmed
¾ cup nonfat skim milk
¼ cup buttermilk
1 cup dark raisins
½ cup chopped walnuts

Position rack in center of oven; preheat oven to 325 degrees F. Lightly grease a 9 x 5 x 3" loaf pan, line with waxed paper, and grease the paper.

In a 2½ quart bowl sift flour, baking powder, baking soda and salt. Stir to blend and make a well in center.

In a 1½ quart bowl whisk egg, butter, honey, milk and buttermilk. Beat well. Stir all at once into flour mixture just until flour is moistened. Gently fold in raisins and walnuts to distribute evenly. Spoon into prepared pan.

Bake at 325 degrees F. for 1 hour 10 minutes, or until a test toothpick inserted in center comes out clean. Let pan stand 10 minutes before turning out bread onto a wire rack to cool. When cool, wrap well.

Makes one 9 x 5 x 3" loaf, about 14 slices.

Each slice contains about: 203 calories, 4.5g protein, 37g carbohydrate, 1.5g fiber, 5g fat, 20mg cholesterol, 164mg sodium.

Love of the Irish

In the past, an Irish woman's claim to good cooking rested on her ability to excel in making a proper loaf of soda bread. With the coming of town bakeries, that standard is not as true as it once was, but it is still a much-appreciated art. In fact, many Irish restaurants have a resident soda-bread baker on the staff.

Staying in bed-and-breakfasts out in the countryside, feasting on traditional Irish breakfasts, you can still enjoy pots of steaming hot strong tea and delicious wedges of freshly baked Irish soda bread served with generous amounts of farm butter and jam. The soda bread at each B&B is usually different in appearance, taste and texture, but all will be delightful, typifying the simple eating pleasures of rural Ireland.

Although there are many types of bread in Ireland, including those leavened with yeast, why is this simple quick-bread considered the definitive Irish loaf? Would it be the weather? Ireland, with its damp and cool climate almost year-round, would not be the best place for yeast to thrive and make bread doughs rise, especially centuries ago when drafty farmhouses were unheated. Non-yeast doughs were easier to handle. Another advantage to soda bread is its simplicity—the Irish woman would go to the local grist mill for coarse-grained flour crushed from old millstones, and probably used soured milk from her own cow and eggs from her hens in the yard; baking soda she would buy at the market on one of her long infrequent walks to the village.

The Irish woman would be sure to score every loaf of soda bread with the mark of the cross, a custom dating back to the Middle Ages when all food was blessed or "crossed" before meals. Some say the cross is also to ensure that the bread turns out successfully; it certainly prevents the loaf from cracking unevenly and helps make it easier to tear into neater wedges.

To bake an authentic loaf, you need the right flour: look for flours with some "body." Some health-food stores carry genuine stone-ground flours; coarse grains and bran are available from companies listed in Appendix 3.

Irish Soda Bread

A handsome whole-wheat loaf, marked with the traditional cross, which makes it easier to break into wedges the Irish call farls. After baking and cooling, store the loaf wrapped in a damp tea towel to keep it moist.

1 cup unbleached all-purpose flour
2 tablespoons granulated sugar
1½ teaspoons baking powder
½ teaspoon *each* salt and baking soda
1 cup whole-wheat flour
¾ teaspoon caraway seed
½ cup dried Zante currants
2 tablespoons cold butter or soy margarine
1 large egg
¾ cup buttermilk

Position rack in center of oven, preheat oven to 375 degrees F., and grease and flour an 8" round baking pan.

In a 2½ quart mixing bowl sift flour, sugar, baking powder, salt and baking soda. Add whole-wheat flour, caraway seed and currants. Stir to blend. Add butter and cut in with a pastry blender or two knives until crumbly.

In a 1½ quart bowl whisk egg slightly and blend in buttermilk; add to dry ingredients and stir until blended. Turn out onto a floured board and knead until smooth, two to three minutes. Shape into a round loaf and press into prepared pan until dough is out to the edge. With a sharp knife, cut a cross on top of loaf, about ½" deep in the middle.

Bake at 375 degrees F. for 35 to 40 minutes. Remove bread from pan and turn out onto a wire rack to cool. Serve in wedges.

Makes 1 loaf, about 8 wedges.

Each wedge serving contains about: 191 calories, 5.5g protein, 34g carbohydrate, 3g fiber, 4g fat, 35mg cholesterol, 309mg sodium.

Lemon Aids

Here's how to squeeze the most out of lemons and limes:

✦ To avoid undesirable chemicals, dyes, pesticides or sprays, buy organically grown fruit.

✦ Wash the fruit in soapy water, rinse well and blot dry with paper towel.

✦ Zest: remove with the fine side of a grater, or a zester tool available in cookware shops. Avoid the white pith which is bitter. Expect about one tablespoon grated zest from one large lemon or two limes.

✦ Grate zest just before use; it becomes tough as it air-dries.

✦ Juice: remove from lemon within a day or two of zesting, since the fruit rapidly deteriorates without the zest covering.

✦ If fruit is chilled, bring it to room temperature or zap in the microwave oven for 20 seconds, for the most juice.

✦ Before cutting and squeezing, roll fruit around on the countertop with the flat of your hand to release the small juice sacs.

✦ Lemon and lime juice will keep in the refrigerator, covered, for up to three days or in the freezer for about one month.

✦ Freeze juice in plastic ice-cube trays. When frozen, toss into plastic food bags and wrap tightly.

Lemon Muffins

After baking these muffins, split them open horizontally and spread lightly with English Lemon Curd Spread, on page 108.

½ cup (1 stick) butter or soy margarine, at room
    temperature
1 cup granulated sugar
2 large eggs
1 ⅔ cups unbleached all-purpose flour
1 teaspoon baking powder
½ teaspoon salt
½ cup nonfat skim milk
½ cup chopped almonds
1 tablespoon finely grated lemon peel
1 teaspoon vanilla extract
English Lemon Curd Spread (optional)

Lightly grease muffin wells, or line with paper cases.

In a 2½ quart mixing bowl beat butter and sugar together until creamy. Add eggs, one at a time, beating well after each addition. Stir together the flour, baking powder and salt, and add alternately with the milk to the creamed mixture. Gently fold in nuts, lemon peel and vanilla extract to distribute evenly. Spoon batter into prepared muffin cups.

Bake in a preheated oven at 350 degrees F. for approximately 30 minutes. Allow muffins to cool 5 minutes before turning out of pan onto a wire rack.

Makes about 12 2½" muffins.

Each muffin (without Lemon Curd Spread) contains about: 244 calories, 4.5g protein, 32g carbohydrate, 1g fiber, 11.5g fat, 56mg cholesterol, 211mg sodium.

English Lemon Curd Spread

As an accompaniment to Lemon Muffins, Lime Tea Loaf, or as a spread on breakfast toast and crispbreads, English Lemon Curd provides a tartness that's a welcome change from sweeter preserves.

After preparing the curd, cover and store it in the refrigerator where it will keep for about two weeks.

½ cup (1 stick) butter or soy margarine
1½ cups granulated sugar
Grated peel (zest) from 2 lemons
Juice from 3 lemons
6 large eggs

Melt butter in a double-boiler top, over hot water, and stir in sugar. Add lemon zest and juice. Whisk eggs slightly, just sufficient to blend yolks with whites, and add to mixture. Stir well, then cook over hot water until thick, stirring occasionally. Pour into hot sterilized jars.

Makes about 2½ cups.

One tablespoon of spread contains about: 62 calories, 1g protein, 8g carbohydrate, 0 fiber, 3g fat, 38mg cholesterol, 33mg sodium.

Lime Tea Loaf

An elegant quick-bread with delicate flavor that is ideal for a special tea, a shower party or bridge luncheon.

3 cups unbleached all-purpose flour
3 teaspoons baking powder
1 teaspoon salt
¼ teaspoon baking soda
¾ cup granulated sugar
1 large egg
1½ cups nonfat skim milk
¼ cup *each* vegetable oil and freshly squeezed lime juice
2 teaspoons grated lime zest

Glaze:
   2 tablespoons granulated sugar
   1 tablespoon lime juice

Position rack in center of oven, preheat oven to 350 degrees F. and lightly grease a 9 x 5 x 3" loaf pan.

In a 2½ quart mixing bowl sift flour, baking powder, salt, baking soda and sugar. Stir to blend and make a well in center.

In a 1½ quart bowl whisk egg, milk, oil, lime juice and lime zest. Beat thoroughly. Add to dry ingredients all at once and stir just until flour is moistened. Pour into prepared loaf pan.

Bake at 350 degrees F. for 1 hour or until test toothpick inserted in center comes out clean. Cool in pan 10 minutes, then turn out onto a wire rack. While loaf is still warm, prick loaf with a fork, make glaze by combining granulated sugar and lime juice, and drizzle glaze into holes.

Makes one 9 x 5 x 3" loaf, about 14 slices.

Each slice (with glaze) contains about: 197 calories, 4g protein, 35g carbohydrate, 1g fiber, 4.5g fat, 16mg cholesterol, 256mg sodium.

Sweet Goodness from the Maple

From late February until well into April, the farmers are tapping the sap from sugar "bushes"—stands of the American tree known botanically as *Acer saccharum*, the sugar maples found primarily in the northeast United States and southeast provinces of Canada. A tree must be at least 40 years old before sap can be drawn, and it takes between 35 and 40 gallons of sap to produce one gallon of syrup.

Fact or fable, the story goes that an Indian squaw was the first to discover the sweetness of maple sap. She was cooking a rabbit one day and, needing some liquid, she caught and used some of the sap seeping from an opening in a maple. Her cooked dish using the sap was so delicious that the tribe decided to tap more trees.

The Iroquois people were the first to set up camps among sugar-maple woods and use their tomahawks to make diagonal gashes in the trunks of the trees. Into each incision they inserted a reed or a concave piece of bark through which the sap was conveyed to a bark trough or hollowed-out log. The sap was brought to a boil by placing fire-heated stones inside the logs, reducing the watery liquid to a syrupy consistency.

Early European settlers substituted wooden spouts for the bark, and replaced the hollowed logs with copper or iron kettles for boiling the sap. The maple business is slow to change in the northern woods, but the primitive gear for sap collection has now been replaced in some more modern orchards with plastic spigots and plastic tubing running sap directly to the "sugar houses." Each of these small wooden sheds is topped by vents that send clouds of sweet-smelling steam from the large evaporator—steam that can be seen and sniffed from miles away. When it's "sugarin' time" in the woods, it means getting together for a sugar party, with good companionship and good food—traditionally home-made bread, dill pickles, and eggs boiled in the sap.

Maple Syrup Muffins

Maple syrup is filtered and graded according to a grading system developed by the Vermont Department of Agriculture. "Fancy" grade is the most delicate in flavor; Grade B is more robust and is usually used in cooking to give the distinctive flavor of maple. Grade C (often only available from the sugar house) is even darker and stronger in flavor.

The maple butter in this recipe is optional, but it makes the perfect accompaniment for these richly flavored muffins.

⅓ cup shortening
½ cup granulated sugar
¾ cup pure maple syrup
2¼ cups unbleached all-purpose flour
3 teaspoons baking powder
½ teaspoon salt
⅓ cup nonfat skim milk
1 large egg, well beaten
1 teaspoon vanilla extract

Maple Butter:

   ½ cup *each* unsalted butter and pure maple syrup

Line muffin wells with paper cases or grease lightly.

In a 2½ quart mixing bowl cream shortening with sugar; stir in syrup.

In a 1½ quart bowl sift flour, baking powder and salt. Add to syrup mixture alternately with milk. Fold in beaten egg and add vanilla extract. Spoon into prepared muffin wells.

Bake in a preheated oven at 350 degrees F. for about 35 minutes. Turn onto a wire rack to cool slightly. Serve with maple butter if desired: beat butter (at room temperature) with maple syrup until well blended.

Makes about 12 2½" muffins.

Each muffin (excluding maple butter) contains about: 228 calories, 3g protein, 40g carbohydrate, 1g fiber, 6.5g fat, 18mg cholesterol, 182mg sodium.

Tofu: Nutritional Jackpot

Since 200 B.C. the Chinese have been producing tofu (also known as bean curd), by soaking dried soybeans, boiling them, separating the pulp and soy "milk." Coagulants are added to the soymilk to separate curds from whey, then the curds are left to firm up in molds to make soft custard-like blocks. In China, tofu is boiled, baked, sautéed, stewed, steamed, deep-fried, stuffed, and even charcoal-grilled and eaten on a stick. In Japan, restaurants called *tofu ryori* specialize in serving course after course of almost nothing but tofu: cold tofu, hot tofu, tofu with dipping sauce, in hot fish broth, or coated with a savory sauce and eaten like a Popsicle.

In the United States, health-food stores generally offer the best selections of several basic types of tofu—soft, regular and firm. Which should you choose? It depends on the recipe you are preparing, and the final texture you want for the dish.

Soft (*Kinugoshi*, or silken): This Japanese style is the softest of all tofu, with a delicate texture that makes it perfect for creamy soups and sauces. It falls apart if stir-fried, unless first weighted and drained. It doesn't readily absorb flavors.

Chinese: Firmer than *kinugoshi*, but still creamy smooth, this one is good in soups and simmered dishes.

Regular (Chinese or Japanese): This type has had more water removed by being pressed longer than soft tofu. Use it the same way as soft tofu, as well as in casseroles and stir-fries.

Firm and extra-firm: This tofu has had even more water drained off. With a definite skin on the outside and a grainy texture on the inside, it is highly nutritious. It still retains its shape after cutting, slicing and dicing, and is a good choice for stir-frying.

Fermented: Regular tofu is allowed to ferment, then steeped in brine with rice wine, salt and spices. It develops a robust flavor, a dense texture, and may have a red or white tint. The white-tinted makes a good addition to salads and vegetables dishes.

Oatmeal Tofu Bread

Tofu is a powerhouse of nutrition—perfect for giving a boost to meatless meals, and a dieter's dream: rich in calcium for building and maintaining strong bones, high in protein, low in fat, cholesterol-free, and it's inexpensive.

1½ cups unbleached all-purpose flour
1 teaspoon *each* baking soda, salt and ground cinnamon
½ teaspoon ground nutmeg
⅔ cup light brown sugar, packed
1 cup coarse oatmeal
2 large eggs
⅓ cup vegetable oil
1 cup soft tofu, drained
1 cup chopped walnuts

Position rack in center of oven, preheat oven to 325 degrees F., and grease a 9 x 5 x 3" loaf pan, or coat with nonstick cooking spray.

In a 2½ quart bowl sift flour, baking soda, salt, cinnamon and nutmeg; add brown sugar and oatmeal. Stir to blend and make a well in center.

In a 1½ quart bowl whisk eggs, oil and tofu. Add to flour mixture and stir just until blended. Gently fold in walnuts to distribute evenly. Spread batter in prepared loaf pan.

Bake at 325 degrees F. for 1 hour or until test toothpick inserted in center comes out clean. Let stand 15 minutes before removing from pan to a wire rack for complete cooling.

Makes one 9 x 5 x 3" loaf, about 14 slices.

Each slice contains about: 236 calories, 6g protein, 26g carbohydrate, 2g fiber, 12.5g fat, 30mg cholesterol, 226mg sodium.

Proper British Marmalade

One of the essentials on every properly laid breakfast table in Britain is a dish of amber-colored tart-flavored marmalade, set beside a silver toast rack carrying thin crisp slices of toast.

Although marmalades can be made with other citrus such as lemon, lime and grapefruit, and even other ingredients such as rhubarb, ginger and apples, the connoisseur would only recognize a preserve containing the bitter Seville oranges, sugar, and nothing else. It is a matter of taste and esthetics whether the marmalade has thin elegant strips of peel distributed through the preserve, or is endowed with thick chunky pieces. The underlying flavor, however, should be one of tartness, perhaps a tinge of bitterness, for the spread that forms part of the first meal of the day. Most households in the British Isles reserve orange marmalade for the breakfast table, eating other sweeter jams and jellies later in the day such as at tea time. But it's not unknown for marmalade to be an ingredient in cakes, quick-breads and tarts, and a rich addition to Christmas plum puddings.

Why is marmalade distinctively British and how did it originate? The Oxford English Dictionary informs us that for centuries marmalade was a concoction made from the *marmelo* (literally, honey-apple), a type of quince. The word marmalade came from the French, meaning fruits that have been stewed for a long time until they become a thick purée.

The invention of bitter orange marmalade apparently came about in the early eighteenth century in the city of Dundee in Scotland. A ship from Spain, carrying a large cargo of oranges from Seville was caught in a storm and took refuge in Dundee harbor. A Mr. James Keiller bought the oranges in quantity, but later discovered the fruit was bitter and realized he would be unable to sell them. However his resourceful wife Janet, not wishing to waste the fruit, made it into a conserve or jam, with the addition of sugar, and so began the manufacture of marmalade which traditionally has been centered in Dundee.

Orange Marmalade Bread

An attractive bread to serve in slices for breakfast, warmed in the toaster, for a delicious start to the day. The marmalade is aromatic and the honey gives moistness. It's best made the day before you need it, to allow easier slicing with less crumbling and for flavors to mellow.

2 cups unbleached all-purpose flour
½ cup whole-wheat flour
4 teaspoons baking powder
1 teaspoon salt
2 large eggs
2 tablespoons vegetable oil
¼ cup mild honey
¾ cup Seville orange marmalade
½ cup nonfat skim milk
¼ cup freshly squeezed orange juice
1 teaspoon grated orange zest
½ cup chopped walnuts

Coat a 9 x 5 x 3" loaf pan with nonstick cooking spray.

In a 2½ quart bowl sift flours, baking powder and salt. Stir to blend and make a well in center.

In a 1½ quart bowl whisk the eggs with oil, honey, marmalade, milk, orange juice and orange zest. Add to flour mixture and stir only until flour is well moistened. Fold in nuts to distribute evenly. Spoon batter into prepared loaf pan.

Bake in a preheated oven at 350 degrees F. for 60 to 70 minutes, until lightly browned, and a test toothpick inserted in center comes out clean. Place a tent of aluminum foil lightly over loaf for last 15 minutes to prevent overbrowning. Cool slightly in pan for 15 minutes before turning onto a wire rack. After cooling, wrap well.

Makes one 9 x 5 x 3" loaf, about 14 slices.

Each slice contains about: 204 calories, 4.5g protein, 36g carbohydrate, 1.5g fiber, 5.5g fat, 30mg cholesterol, 264mg sodium.

Passion Fruit

As we pay greater attention to health and nutrition, it's fun to discover delicious new fruits to increase our intake of complex carbohydrates, fiber and vitamins. Although passion fruit were formerly considered uncommon in the United States, better supplies are arriving in stores from local and New Zealand growers, so that they should be available year-round. Look for them at farmers' markets where they will probably be organically grown.

Native to Brazil, Paraguay and northern Argentina, passion fruit come in two distinct forms: the purple, subtropical type most likely to be found in U.S. markets (known as lilikoi in Hawaii), and yellow or golden tropical varieties sometimes available (especially in Hawaii).

The fruit is extremely ugly on the outside, purple-brown, wrinkled and egg-shaped. Inside the tough shell, however, is brilliant yellow, jelly-like pulp and black seeds, with a bright lemony-tart flavor—distinctive, tropical, fragrant and highly concentrated. When shopping for passion fruit, choose those that are creased and wrinkled but not cracked. Even when fully ripened, the shell remains firm and hard.

Although passion fruit can be expensive when bought individually, if you come across bargain prices, it pays to buy a good supply and freeze them in plastic bags. Well-wrapped in plastic, they freeze well for months. In the refrigerator they last for about a week once fully ripened.

Few passion fruit are grown in the United States (Hawaii, Florida and California), but where they are produced in quantity in tropical and subtropical countries such as Australia, New Zealand, South and Central America, Kenya, South Africa and southeast Asia, cooks use them in prodigious amounts in ice creams and sherbets, cake fillings and pies, gelatins and sauces.

No, the fruit isn't known to be an aphrodisiac, and the name doesn't derive from any romantic passion it might arouse. It originated from the Passions of Christ: the various parts of the lovely flowers appear to resemble the crown of thorns, crucifixion nails and wounds.

Passion Fruit Bran Muffins

The black seeds look attractive in the muffins and give a delightful crunch. Leaving the seeds in the pulp during preparation is preferable, to provide a greater amount of fiber, but if you want to remove seeds (a tedious job), squeeze the pulp through a sieve or two thicknesses of cheesecloth.

3 passion fruit
About ¾ cup nonfat skim milk
1 large egg
¼ cup (½ stick) melted butter or soy margarine
Grated zest of 1 lemon
1 cup bran cereal (granules, not flakes)
1 cup unbleached all-purpose flour
½ cup granulated sugar
2 teaspoons baking powder
½ teaspoon baking soda

Cut tips off passion fruit with a sharp knife. Spoon pulp including seeds into a measuring cup (should measure about ¼ cup), and fill measure with enough milk to make 1 cup.

In a 1½ quart bowl whisk egg, butter, lemon zest and passion fruit/milk mixture. Stir in bran, then set aside for 10 minutes to allow bran to soften.

Position rack in center of oven, preheat oven to 400 degrees F. and line muffin wells with paper cases.

In a 2½ quart bowl sift flour, sugar, baking powder and baking soda. Stir to blend and make a well in center. Add bran/milk mixture all at once and stir until flour is just moistened. Spoon into prepared muffin wells.

Bake at 400 degrees F. for about 25 minutes, or until golden brown. Cool muffins in pan 5 minutes before turning out onto a wire rack. Serve warm.

Makes about 12 2½" muffins.

Each muffin contains about: 138 calories, 3.5g protein, 24g carbohydrate, 3g fiber, 4.5g fat, 28mg cholesterol, 223mg sodium.

The Peanut Butter Story

For bread spreads, the British think marmalade is marvelous, the French choose chocolate, Australians value their Vegemite—and Americans prefer peanut butter.

During the Second World War, American GIs would generously give cherished jars of peanut butter to their British host families and girlfriends, and the spread was gratefully accepted in those times of food rationing. But peanut butter never really caught on with the British. And the French, who appreciate the *oil* from peanuts for its delicate flavor and ability to cook at high temperatures, have tended to look askance at peanut butter.

Yet generations of Americans grow up with peanut butter, and consider it a lunch-box essential, spread on bread with jelly, jam or (President Clinton's preference) bananas. Mothers rely on it as cheap nourishment for their families; for children, it's a favorite comfort food they never outgrow. By the time of high school graduation the average child has eaten 1,500 peanut-butter sandwiches!

Peanut butter's inventor seems to be somewhat of a mystery. George Washington Carver (1864-1943), the agricultural chemist and educator in Tuskegee, Alabama, developed 300 uses for peanuts; was he the first to make the spread? Or was the originator Dr. John Harvey Kellogg of Battle Creek (Michigan) Sanitarium, experimenting with peanuts as a vegetarian protein for his patients? Or one of Kellogg's employees, Joseph Lambert, who sold his own hand-operated peanut-butter grinders in 1896? Or perhaps it was an unknown St. Louis doctor who concocted it (using nothing but ground roasted nuts) in 1890? Or Ambrose W. Straub of St. Louis who in 1903 patented a peanut-butter machine? Or C. H. Sumner who sold the stuff at the 1904 World's Fair in St. Louis?

Whichever anecdote you believe, about twenty years after the World's Fair, peanut butter's popularity had spread: women were making tiny batches at home, using small ovens and hand grinders. Today's huge production is all mechanized; we eat 800 million pounds of it annually, and membership is increasing in the Adult Peanut Butter Lovers Fan Club!

Peanut Butter Apple Bread

Combine America's favorite spread and favorite fruit, and you've got a quick-loaf that's a winner. This is a hearty snacking bread that children of all ages will love, at all times of the day.

½ cup dry-roasted unsalted peanuts
1 large red apple
1⅞ cups unbleached all-purpose flour
1½ teaspoons ground cinnamon
1 teaspoon baking soda
½ teaspoon salt
⅓ cup *each* light brown and granulated sugars
2 large eggs
¼ cup vegetable oil (preferably peanut)
⅓ cup apple juice (or more, depending on juiciness of
    apple)
½ cup creamy-style peanut butter

Position rack in center of oven, preheat oven to 350 degrees F., and lightly grease a 9 x 5 x 3" loaf pan.

Measure peanuts, chop finely, and set aside. Core apple but leave skin intact; dice very small (should make 1 cup), and set aside.

In a 2½ quart mixing bowl sift flour, cinnamon, baking soda and salt. Add sugars, stir to blend and make a well in center.

In a 1½ quart bowl whisk eggs, oil, apple juice and peanut butter. Beat thoroughly till blended and smooth. Add all at once to flour mixture and stir just until flour is moistened. Fold in chopped nuts and apple dice. Spread in prepared loaf pan.

Bake at 350 degrees F. for about 55 minutes, or until a test toothpick inserted in center comes out clean. To prevent over-browning, place a tent of aluminum foil over loaf for last 15 minutes of baking. Let bread cool in pan for about 30 minutes before turning out onto a wire rack to cool completely. When cool, wrap well. For easy slicing, serve the following day.

Makes one 9 x 5 x 3" loaf, about 16 slices.

Each slice contains about: 210 calories, 5.5g protein, 25g carbohydrate, 2g fiber, 10.5g fat, 26mg cholesterol, 166mg sodium.

All-American Peanuts

Several hundred names exist for the peanut. Among the most popular are *cacahuete*, earth almond, earth nut, earth pistachio, grass nut and monkey nut. But they are *not* nuts. And although signs at the Democratic Convention nominating President Jimmy Carter declared, "Make the peanut our national tree," peanuts *do not* grow on trees. They grow below ground from leguminous plants related to peas, so that a more realistic name would be "ground peas."

Peanuts are native to South America, probably Peru, where they have been found in ancient tombs and depicted on pre-Columbian Andean pottery. Early trade routes took them north to Mexico, and then native tribes in North America cultivated them; so when the first European colonists arrived in Virginia they found them there.

Spanish explorers in the 1600s introduced them from the Americas into China via the Malay Peninsula, after which many countries around the world enjoyed peanuts in different forms in their cuisine, tossing them into stir-fried dishes, pressing them into oil, and grinding them into flavorful pastes and sauces.

Meanwhile Portuguese slavers took peanuts from Brazil and planted them on the West African coast as a cheap nourishing food supply for captives waiting for ships to the New World. Peanuts became a staple in African cuisine, where they were renamed "ground nuts." Black slaves referred to them as "goober" (*nguba* from the Gedda dialect), a name they brought to America—although few people know of its African origin.

Colonists in America up to this time had just been using peanuts to feed hogs, but when black Africans were put to work on cotton and tobacco plantations, the slaves grew them in small patches and cooked with them as they had in Africa.

During the Civil War, Confederate troops used peanuts as a cheap coffee substitute. But it was probably Union soldiers who popularized peanuts beyond the Southern states when the young men with no other employment would hawk bags of freshly roasted nuts on the streets of Northern cities.

Peanut Oatmeal Favorites

These muffins, with a hint of spice, are best eaten fresh on the day you bake them, since the delicious crunch of the nuts is apt to soften later. Toss a small green salad as an accompaniment, and you have a light but satisfying lunch.

1 cup coarse oatmeal
1 cup nonfat skim milk with 1 tablespoon mild vinegar
1 large egg
½ cup light brown sugar
¼ cup vegetable oil
¼ cup creamy-style peanut butter
1 cup unbleached all-purpose flour
1 teaspoon baking soda
½ teaspoon *each* baking powder and ground cinnamon
½ cup chopped dry-roasted lightly salted peanuts

In a 2½ quart mixing bowl stir together oatmeal and milk/vinegar mixture and let soak for 1 hour. Whisk in egg, brown sugar, oil and peanut butter, and beat thoroughly.

Position rack in center of oven, preheat oven to 400 degrees F., and line muffin wells with paper cases.

In a 1½ quart bowl sift flour, baking soda, baking powder and cinnamon, and stir to blend. Mix into oatmeal mixture just until flour is moistened and blended. Gently fold in peanuts to distribute evenly. Spoon into prepared muffin wells until two-thirds full.

Bake at 400 degrees F. for 20 to 25 minutes until golden brown. Allow to cool 5 minutes in pan before turning out onto a wire rack.

Makes about 12 2½" muffins.

Each muffin contains about: 219 calories, 6g protein, 25g carbo-hydrate, 2g fiber, 11g fat, 18mg cholesterol, 136mg sodium.

'Fire of Zeus'

Botanists named the persimmon genus *Diospyros*, "fire of Zeus," and it's easy to see why when the spectacular orange-red fruit are a flaming blaze of color, hanging on often-bare trees at the end of fall. The flamboyant persimmon is beautifully sweet when ripe.

Native Americans of the Algonquin tribe would relish eating the ripe fruit (*D. virginiana*) wherever they fell after the first frost, or collect them for drying to enjoy later in the winter, thus giving us the word persimmon from *pessemmin*, "dried fruit." Indians made a sort of bread by mixing the pulp with crushed corn kernels, so early colonists adopted the custom too by using persimmon pulp in their baking; American colonizers of the seventeenth century also discovered, after their crops of barley and hops had failed, that persimmons could make a "very potable" fermented beer.

After 1853, when Commodore Matthew Perry returned from an expedition to Japan, the United States Department of Agriculture subsequently imported thousands of persimmon grafts of the Hachiya variety (*D. kaki*), native to China, Japan and the Himalayas, because it was less astringent. It is this fruit which makes up 90 percent of commercial plantings in California, Florida and Texas, and the one you'll see most often in markets between September and November.

If you have your own persimmon tree, you probably know that fruit is best left on it to ripen naturally before use; however supermarket chains generally ship Hachiya persimmons while they're still hard. Look for fruit that is bright orange-red—a few black spots don't affect quality—but don't attempt to eat underripe fruit (it will make your mouth pucker and cause stomach cramps). Place too-firm fruit in a bag with a ripe apple or banana, close the bag and leave at room temperature for several days while the natural ethylene gas ripens and softens the fruit. Use immediately, or refrigerate and use within a few days.

Persimmon Loaf

A luscious blend of sweet spice, fruit and nuts folded into the quick-bread batter, with a splash of whiskey, make this a popular loaf to enjoy during the holiday season.

2 very ripe medium-size Hachiya persimmons
1¾ cups unbleached all-purpose flour
1 cup granulated sugar
1 teaspoon baking soda
½ teaspoon ground mace
2 large eggs
½ cup (1 stick) melted butter or soy margarine
⅓ cup bourbon
1 cup finely chopped walnuts

Position rack in center of oven, preheat oven to 350 degrees F. and grease and flour two 1-pound coffee cans.

Wash and dry persimmons. Cut off stem-end and halve fruit. Do not remove skin, but discard any seeds. Place in a food processor and purée (should be about 1 cup purée).

In a 2½ quart mixing bowl sift flour, sugar, salt, baking soda and mace. Stir to blend and make a well in center.

In a 1½ quart bowl whisk eggs, and add melted butter, persimmon purée and bourbon. Beat thoroughly. Add to flour mixture and stir just until blended. Fold in walnuts. Spoon into prepared coffee cans until three-fourths full.

Bake at 350 degrees F. for about 1 hour or until a cake tester inserted in centers comes out clean. Cool in the cans for 30 minutes before turning onto a wire rack. When completely cooled, slice and spread with softened cream cheese.

Makes two loaves, about 16 slices.

Each slice (excluding cream cheese) contains about: 233 calories, 3.5g protein, 28g carbohydrate, 1g fiber, 11g fat, 42mg cholesterol, 119mg sodium.

Pineapple: King of Fruits

After seeing the blue-green spiky plants flourishing in neat regimented rows on the islands of Hawaii, many people are surprised to learn the fruit is not a native. In the Hawaiian language, pineapple is called *halakahiki*, "foreign fruit," and known as the "King of Fruits" because of its crown.

In the fifteenth century, the Spaniards discovered pineapples all over the Caribbean islands and later in Central and South America as well. De Soto sampled pineapples in the West Indies; the men from Magellan's ships while resting in Brazil in 1519 found "sweet pineapples, a very delectable fruit"; and in 1595 Sir Walter Raleigh reported an abundance of them growing in Guiana. Carib Indians hung pineapples at their hut entrances as a symbol of welcome (a sign adopted later by New Englanders as a decoration on furniture).

When ships left the Americas, sea captains took pineapples as provision against scurvy, and after eating the fruit, the crews planted discarded crowns wherever ships touched land. In this way, the Portuguese took them to India, the East Indies including the island of Java, and to ports along the slave routes between Brazil and Africa.

When Europeans first saw the fruit, they thought they resembled pine cones, calling them "pines of the Indies." The English added "apple" to denote a juicy delicious fruit.

Americans only became aware of them on rare visits to the West Indies: when George Washington went to Barbados in 1751 and encountered many hitherto-unknown fruits, he wrote "none pleases my taste as does the pine." However, even until the end of the nineteenth century, the fruit was to remain a foreign curiosity for most people.

How did pineapple reach the Pacific? Some believe an off-course Spanish ship traveling the trade route between Acapulco and the Philippines was responsible for accidentally introducing pineapples in the Pacific, even before Captain Cook brought them to the islands in about 1777. The pineapple industry in Hawaii didn't begin until 1882 when Captain John Kidwell imported 1,000 slips from South American plants, and in 1892 began canning operations.

Pineapple Muffins (Fresh Pineapple)

When choosing a fresh pineapple, look for a crown of fresh-looking green leaves and a body that is firm, not soft. The color of the shell is not necessarily an indication of its maturity, as a very green pineapple may be a "green shell"—fully ripe but with little or no yellowing. To prepare pineapple, twist or slice off crown. With a sharp knife, cut lengthwise into halves then quarters; trim away ends and fibrous core. Remove fruit from shell with a curved knife and cut into chunks.

1 cup finely chopped fresh pineapple
1⅞ cups unbleached all-purpose flour
2 teaspoons baking powder
½ teaspoon *each* baking soda, salt and ground cloves
½ cup granulated sugar
1 large egg
1 cup nonfat skim milk
¼ cup (½ stick) melted butter or soy margarine

Chop pineapple, drain off juice and set aside.

Position rack in center of oven, preheat oven to 400 degrees F., and line muffin wells with paper cases.

In a 2½ quart mixing bowl sift flour, baking powder, baking soda, salt, ground cloves and sugar. Stir to blend and make a well in center.

In a 1½ pint bowl whisk egg, milk and butter; pour into flour mixture. Stir just until flour is moistened. Gently fold in drained pineapple. Spoon into prepared muffin wells.

Bake at 400 degrees F. for 20 to 25 minutes or until a test toothpick inserted in centers comes out clean.

Makes about 12 2½" muffins.

Each muffin contains about: 158 calories, 3g protein, 26g carbohydrate, 1g fiber, 4.5g fat, 28mg cholesterol, 233mg sodium.

Lanai: The Pineapple Island

One of the legends in the State of Hawaii is that Lanai, the "Pineapple Isle" was once haunted by evil spirits and avoided by native people. Although a young prince banished the evil ones to make the island a safer place to live, it was still too inhospitable because of a lack of water, and only used to exile women who had committed *tapu*.

When nineteenth century Morman settlers attempted to establish ranches on the island, they failed because wild goats, sheep and cattle had stripped the soil bare. At the beginning of the twentieth century, the Lanai Company planted trial plots of sugar beets, hoping to establish a sugar industry, but again a lack of water prevented a successful operation, and another venture failed.

Then in 1924, after an investment of $1 million to develop water resources, the Hawaiian Pineapple Company, under the leadership of James Dole, started its Lanai operations. Development was difficult because the company had to clear away land choked with cacti, and cope with incessant tradewinds sweeping away the arid soil. But as roads, reservoirs and a safe harbor were built, the new plantings gradually became successful. In the 1930s and 1940s the plantations prospered and the population tripled, until Lanai became the largest plantation in the world with highly-paid workers. Later, however, because of union difficulties, companies dispersed some of their operations to the Philippines, Thailand and Kenya.

Fruit for canning must be fully ripened on the plant before it is picked and placed on conveyor belts by the field workers. Although the fruit naturally ripens in summertime, growers induce flowering artificially at varying times during the year so that harvesting can proceed all year to ensure steady supplies to the canneries. The largest pineapple cannery in the world is the Dole facility in Honolulu, servicing plantations on Lanai and Oahu, where up to two million fruits arrive each day at peak season. There they are rapidly processed: intricate machines with sharp revolving cylindrical blades cut the shell from the washed fruit, chop off ends and cores—then prepare the familiar slices, chunks and crushed pieces.

Pineapple Treasures (Canned Pineapple)

Sweet taste from the tropics! These muffins make a delightful accompaniment to a chilled fruit platter for a light summer lunch, served with tall frosty glasses of iced tea.

¾ cup crushed pineapple, canned in natural juice
Juice from drained pineapple plus nonfat
    skim milk to measure ¾ cup
2 cups unbleached all-purpose flour
1 teaspoon *each* baking powder and baking soda
½ teaspoon salt
½ cup light brown sugar
1 large egg
½ teaspoon almond extract
¼ cup (½ stick) melted butter or soy margarine
⅓ cup blanched almonds, finely chopped

Position rack in center of oven. Preheat oven to 400 degrees F., and line muffin wells with paper cases.

Drain pineapple. Put juice into measuring cup and add nonfat skim milk to measure ¾ cup. Set aside.

In a 2½ quart bowl sift flour, baking powder, baking soda, and salt. Add brown sugar. Stir to blend and make a well in center.

In a 1½ quart bowl whisk egg with almond extract, juice/milk and butter. Beat thoroughly. Stir into flour mixture until flour is moistened. Fold in crushed pineapple. Spoon into prepared muffin wells. Sprinkle tops with chopped almonds.

Bake at 400 degrees F. for 20 to 25 minutes or until a test toothpick inserted in centers comes out clean.

Makes about 12 2½" muffins.

Each muffin contains about: 185 calories, 4g protein, 29g carbohydrate, 1g fiber, 6.5g fat, 28mg cholesterol, 238mg sodium.

The Forgotten Fruit

Although ancient Greeks couldn't have been aware that a quince is packed with natural pectin, a good source of fiber and vitamin C, they knew, grew, cooked and appreciated this native of Persia and Anatolia. While cultivating it, they grafted improved varieties from Cydonia, Crete, which was said to produce the finest quinces of the ancient world; the Romans referred to it as the Cydonian apple (from which botanists derived its modern scientific label *Cydonia oblonga* or *C. vulgaris*).

For the Greeks, the quince symbolized love, happiness and fertility, so that when an Athenian groom was taking his bride to her new home, well-wishers tossed quinces into the chariot, and flavored the wedding cake with honey, sesame and a quince, to ensure a "fruitful" marriage.

By the sixteenth century the best were considered to be those from Portugal, where the people called them *marmelo* (literally, honey-apple), and produced the first marmalades. Several marmalade recipes published in 1669 in Britain specified quinces; the use of bitter oranges in marmalades did not occur until about a hundred years later.

Quinces were popular in the American colonies: lists of items that settlers wanted brought back from England in 1648 and 1669 included quince seeds; the trees in Virginia were said to produce abundant crops. In New England, the quince was grown not only commercially but also in home gardens, with housewives preserving the fruit as quince "cheese," jelled by all-day boiling to make simple "marmalade." Since the quince is related to the apple and pear, it's not surprising that the flavor and texture of these fresh fruits are similar, but the quince differs because it *must* be cooked. In its raw state the flesh is hard, astringent and indigestible.

The quince is a good example of how different foods become popular and then almost fade from the culinary scene; although centuries ago the fruit was well known and much used, these days there are few producing trees. But with a fresh look at the good nutrition packed into the quince, perhaps the time has come for its revival.

Quince Honey Tea Cake

A honey of a loaf—golden brown, accented with raisins, perfumed delicately with honey and the intriguing taste of quince.

1 medium quince
1 tablespoon *each* mild honey, lemon juice and water
2 cups unbleached all-purpose flour
1 tablespoon baking powder
½ teaspoon *each* baking soda and salt
1 large egg
¼ cup (½ stick) melted butter or soy margarine
½ cup mild honey
½ cup nonfat skim milk
2 teaspoons vanilla extract
1 teaspoon grated lemon zest
⅔ cup golden raisins

With a sharp knife, quarter and peel the quince. Remove core, seeds and hard membranes, and slice each quarter into 8 to 10 slices. Spread slices in a microwavable dish, drizzle with honey, lemon juice and water. Cover dish and microwave on HIGH for 5 minutes. Stir and heat 3 minutes more, or until slices are tender. Purée. Makes about ½ cup. Set aside.

Position rack in center of conventional oven; preheat oven to 325 degrees F. Grease a 9 x 5 x 3" loaf pan, line with waxed paper, and lightly grease paper.

In a 2½ quart bowl sift flour, baking powder, baking soda and salt. Stir to blend and make a well in center.

In a 1½ quart bowl whisk egg, butter, honey, milk, vanilla extract, lemon zest and quince purée. Add to flour mixture and stir just until blended. Fold in golden raisins to distribute evenly. Spread in prepared loaf pan.

Bake at 325 degrees F. for about 1 hour or until a test toothpick inserted in center comes out clean. Let stand 15 minutes before removing from pan onto a wire rack for complete cooling.

Makes one 9 x 5 x 3" loaf, about 14 slices.

Each slice contains about: 172 calories, 3g protein, 33g carbohydrate, 1.5g fiber, 4g fat, 24mg cholesterol, 221mg sodium.

The Cinnamon Story

Cinnamon candies, cinnamon sugar, cinnamon toast, cinnamon rolls, cinnamon buns, cinnamon perfuming warm apple pie, puddings and spiced tea—America adores the spice that finds its way into almost everything good! This warming spice has inviting aroma and irresistible flavor!

We casually shop at the market and pick up a jar of cinnamon sticks or a small tin of ground cinnamon for a dollar or so, and yet a few centuries ago men were endangering their lives to obtain the then costly spice. Merchants controlled the spice trade in the Middle East, with overland caravan routes closely guarded and sources kept secret. The Arabs weren't about to divulge the fact that cinnamon trees were growing wild in western India, Ceylon and southeast Asia.

As part of their control of the spice market, traders would create myths and legends to exaggerate the difficulties, boost their prices, and fend off attempts by others to reach the precious bark. Herodotus recorded this incredible tale of the way Arabs said they collected cinnamon:

"Where it comes from and what country produces it, they do not know. What they say is that the dry sticks, which we have learned from the Phoenicians to call cinnamon, are brought by large birds which carry them to their nests made of mud, on mountain precipices which no man can climb.

"The method the Arabians have invented for getting hold of them is to cut up the bones of dead oxen or donkeys, or other animals, into very large joints which they carry to the spot in question and leave on the ground near the nests. They then retire to a safe distance and the birds fly down and carry off the joints of meat to their nests which, not being strong enough to bear the weight, break and fall to the ground. Then the men come along and pick up the cinnamon. ..."

In order to break the control, adventurers fitted out sailing ships to seek sea passages to the spice islands of the Indies. In doing so, they discovered new worlds and made history.

Ragamuffins!

A bit of word play, to be sure: an attention-getter and conversation-starter. Spiced with cinnamon, spiked with pepper, and topped with red candies resembling holly berries, these muffins look attractive on a plate surrounded by Christmas greenery—a popular choice for holiday buffets and children's parties. Yes, that's pepper included in the ingredients, inspired by European pfefferneuse *cookies.*

1¾ cups unbleached all-purpose flour
½ cup granulated sugar
2 teaspoons baking powder
1 teaspoon ground cinnamon
½ teaspoon *each* salt, ground cloves and white pepper
1 teaspoon grated orange peel
½ teaspoon fennel seeds
1 large egg
1 cup nonfat skim milk
⅓ cup (⅔ stick) melted butter or soy margarine
½ cup confectioners' sugar
Few drops lemon juice
1 oz cinnamon hot candies

Line muffin wells with paper cases.

Sift together first seven ingredients in a 2½ quart mixing bowl. Add orange peel and fennel. Stir to blend and make a well in center.

In a 1½ quart bowl whisk egg, milk and butter, then add all at once to flour mixture. Stir just until flour is moistened and blended. Spoon into prepared muffin wells.

Bake in a preheated oven at 400 degrees F. for 20 minutes. Remove to a wire rack. While still warm, lightly glaze muffins (confectioners' sugar moistened with a few drops lemon juice). Press 5 or 6 candies into glaze on each muffin. Serve promptly.

Makes about 12 2½" muffins.

Each muffin contains about: 178 calories, 3g protein, 29g carbohydrate, 1g fiber, 6g fat, 32mg cholesterol, 212mg sodium.

Reasons for Raisins

There are several good reasons for including dried fruit in baking: sun-dried and packed without preservatives, raisins are a concentrated form of food energy, and a wholesome way to satisfy a sweet tooth; digesting the natural fruit sugars is easy; Nature packages them with fiber and a number of vitamins and minerals; they have no cholesterol and virtually no fat; and they give baked goods moistness and improved keeping qualities.

So what are they? Raisins are grapes with about 85 percent of their moisture extracted, leaving a concentration of goodness and nutrients. Between four and five pounds of grapes produces one pound of raisins.

In the stores you generally find four types of raisins: *dark*, sun-dried, derived from Thompson Seedless grapes; *golden*, oven-dried, from the same grapes, but with a slight tart-sweet flavor; *muscat*—large, dark, sun-dried, from Muscat of Alexandria grapes, with an especially fruity flavor; and *Zante currants* (unrelated to currant berries)—dark, tiny, sun-dried, from Black Corinth grapes.

Raisins are in supermarkets year-round; stock up if you find an economical buy, because sealed packages keep well for up to two years if kept cool. Once you open a package, place the fruit in a screw-top jar (such as a clean dry mayonnaise jar) and store in the refrigerator. Stored in the freezer, they will keep almost indefinitely.

If raisins become hard because of poor storage, simply soften them by placing in a colander, cover, and set over boiling water to steam for up to 5 minutes.

When you want to distribute raisins evenly in muffins, or if you have insufficient for a recipe, it's a good idea to chop them: lightly coat blades of food processor with nonstick cooking spray, for easy clean-up, then chop one-half cup of raisins at a time.

For rich-tasting raisins, soak them in brandy, rum, Sherry, liqueurs or fruit juices: place them in a small saucepan with the liquor and bring to the boil. Remove from heat, cover, and let stand 30 minutes until plump and flavorful.

Raisin Brandy Muffins

When you're looking for an impressive stylish muffin to serve for a holiday meal or special occasion, this is the one.

½ cup dark seedless raisins
¼ cup brandy (or apple juice)
1½ cups bran cereal (granules not flakes)
¾ cup nonfat skim milk
1 large egg
⅓ cup (⅔ stick) melted butter or soy margarine
1½ cups unbleached all-purpose flour
½ cup granulated sugar
3 teaspoons baking powder
1 teaspoon *each* salt and ground cinnamon

Place raisins and brandy in a small saucepan and bring to a boil. Remove from heat, cover, and let stand 30 minutes.

Lightly grease muffin wells, or coat with nonstick cooking spray.

In a 1½ quart bowl soak bran cereal with milk for 5 minutes. Whisk in egg and butter.

In a 2½ quart bowl sift flour, sugar, baking powder, salt and cinnamon. Stir to blend and make a well in center. Add bran/milk mixture. Stir just until flour is moistened. Add raisins and brandy. Mix gently. Spoon into prepared muffin wells.

Bake in a preheated oven at 400 degrees F. for about 25 minutes until golden brown. Turn onto a wire rack to cool slightly.

Makes about 12 2½" muffins.

Each muffin contains about: 203 calories, 4.5g protein, 36g carbohydrate, 4g fiber, 6g fat, 32mg cholesterol, 447mg sodium.

An Orchid for the Baker

Vanilla orchid vines grow plentifully in Mexico, particularly in and around Papantlá in the State of Veracruz, where vanilla growing is an integral part of life. The Totonac workers hand-pick the seed pods when they are slightly underripe and still green, then leave them for three to six months to cure by alternate drying and sweating, to develop their marvelous aroma, flavor, and dark brown or almost black color.

According to Aztec legend, a general Tlacaetl on a mission to capture six young virgins for King Montezuma came upon a wonderful aroma. Tlacaetl was so enchanted by the vanilla fragrance that he returned home not with young maidens but several bean-laden branches of the fabulous plant. Lucky for Tlacaetl, Montezuma and his people were also impressed with the perfume, richness and pungency of the pod they dubbed *ixtlilxochitl* ("black flower" in the Nahuatl dialect); when they mixed chopped vanilla beans with chocolate, they found it enhanced the enjoyment of their customary after-dinner drink.

When Spaniards later arrived in the New World, they too prized the fragrant pod, called it *vainilla*, and brought it back to Europe where it was immediately popular. Thomas Jefferson discovered the delights of vanilla during a visit to France, so after returning to the United States in 1789, he requested the American *chargé d'affaires* in Paris to "send me a packet of 50 pods"—probably the first imported to America.

For three centuries, the Mexicans and Spaniards guarded vanilla cultivation, keeping pod prices high, but in 1829, the French smuggled out cuttings to the tiny French-owned island of Bourbon (now known as Réunion) in the Indian Ocean. At first, their venture was unsuccessful: vanilla flowers formed no pods because the plants are not self-pollinating. Spies later sent to Mexico discovered that the pollen is transferred from stamen to pistil by *Melipona* bees and by hummingbirds (found only in the Americas, and known by some as "Vanilla Birds"). The French solved their problem, however, by skillfully hand pollinating each flower, using delicate touches of a bamboo splinter the size and shape of a hummingbird's beak. This tiny instrument broke control of the vanilla market.

Spicy Classics

The richness of vanilla and spice, and the malted flavor of the cereal, combine to make these praise-winners. Your family will say they're fantastic, and you'll feel good that they're eating wholesome snacks.

1 cup Grape-Nuts cereal
1¼ cups nonfat skim milk
1 large egg
¼ cup (½ stick) melted butter or soy margarine
1 teaspoon vanilla extract
1 cup unbleached all-purpose flour
½ cup granulated sugar
2 teaspoons baking powder
½ teaspoon *each* salt and ground cinnamon
½ cup *each* dark raisins and chopped walnuts

In a 1½ quart microwavable bowl heat cereal and milk in microwave oven on HIGH for 2 minutes. Allow to cool and soften for about 10 minutes. Whisk in egg, butter and vanilla extract. Beat well until smooth.

Line muffin wells with paper cases.

In a 2½ quart mixing bowl sift flour, sugar, baking powder, salt and cinnamon. Stir to blend and make a well in center. Add cereal mixture and stir just until flour is moistened. Gently fold in raisins and walnuts to distribute evenly. Spoon into prepared muffin wells.

Bake in a preheated oven at 400 degrees F. for 20 to 25 minutes, until tops are golden brown. Turn onto a wire rack.

Makes about 12 2½" muffins.

Each muffin contains about: 204 calories, 4.5g protein, 31g carbohydrate, 2g fiber, 7.5g fat, 28mg cholesterol, 268mg sodium.

When Is a Yam Not a Yam?

When it's in the United States. What we cook in America is the sweet potato, whether it's the light-skinned dry-fleshed variety or the dark-skinned moist-fleshed kind. Some people call the dark-skinned type a yam, but this is where the confusion comes in.

Say "yam" outside the United States and it refers to a completely different vegetable: a scruffy, hairy brown tuber shaped like a log; the flesh of a true yam is crisp, sticky and an off-white or yellow tint. True yams are neither related to potatoes or sweet potatoes nor are they sweet or orange color. Yams come from a very specific plant commonly grown in the Caribbean, Africa and tropical Asia.

To explain: Georgia and North Carolina were the States where sweet potatoes (in the morning-glory family) were grown and—correctly—called sweet potatoes. They preferred the light-skinned varieties such as Centennial, Porto Rico, and Jewel. In the early 1930s a new variety called Garnet was developed at Louisiana State University; darker color and more moist after cooking, it was called a yam to differentiate it from other sweet potatoes (derived from the slave name for sweet potatoes *nyami*, "to eat" in Fulani, a language of northwestern and central Africa). Now another dark variety called Beauregard is edging out the Garnet.

Although cooks may argue about the name, there is full agreement among health experts that the sweet potato is packed with nutrition: like other yellow and orange vegetables, it's a good source of vitamins A and C and potassium. Canned sweet potatoes, however, are not as high in nutrients as fresh, due to the processing they undergo, and they generally have added sodium.

When choosing sweet potatoes, look for firm, smooth tubers of uniform shape and color. Select the light-skinned varieties for mashing, as they will be lighter and fluffier; choose the dark-skinned types for cooking whole. Use them within 3 or 4 days of purchase. Keep them dry during storage; never refrigerate them before cooking as cold temperatures cause damage and affect the quality.

Sweet Potato Specials

*Whether baked, glazed, mashed or stuffed, sweet potatoes are sure to find
a place in menu planning about Thanksgiving and Christmas time, when
the bulk of the annual crop is available. They are a natural for including in
muffins and breads for the holiday season.*

*Variation: instead of 3/4 cup milk, substitute ½ cup milk and ¼ cup
cream Sherry.*

1 large sweet potato
1¾ cups unbleached all-purpose flour
¼ cup granulated sugar
3 teaspoons baking powder
½ teaspoon salt
¼ cup light brown sugar
2 teaspoons grated orange peel
1 large egg
¼ cup (½ stick) melted butter or soy margarine
¾ cup nonfat skim milk
½ cup coarsely chopped walnuts

Cut sweet potato into large chunks. Cook in boiling water
for 20 minutes or until tender. Drain well. Remove skin. Process in food blender to a smooth purée (should make ¾ cup).
Set aside to cool.

Line muffin wells with paper cases.

In a 2½ quart mixing bowl sift flour, granulated sugar, baking powder and salt. Add light brown sugar and orange peel.
Stir to blend and make a well in center.

In a 1½ quart bowl whisk egg, butter, milk and cooled
purée, and beat thoroughly. Add to flour mixture and stir just
until flour is moistened. Fold in walnuts to distribute evenly.
Spoon into prepared muffin wells.

Bake in a preheated oven at 400 degrees F. for about 20 to 25
minutes, until a test toothpick inserted in centers comes out
clean. Turn out of pan and cool on a wire rack.

Makes about 12 2½" muffins.

*Each muffin contains about: 191 calories, 4g protein, 28g carbo-
hydrate, 1g fiber, 7.5g fat, 28mg cholesterol, 227mg sodium.*

Nuts About Walnuts

Unless you have access to a walnut orchard, you may never have seen the green "golf balls" on the 50- or 60-foot trees, or recognized them as fresh walnuts. Walnuts are primarily grown in the San Joaquin and Sacramento Valleys of California; Stockton is known as the "Walnut Capital of the World."

When the nuts are ripe enough to split the green husk, a machine fixed to the tree limbs shakes them loose. Workers pick up the fallen nuts and take them to a processing center where the green hulls are removed. The nuts (still in their shells) are dried for five to six hours in oven-like dehydrators, then sorted for sale either in-shell or out.

Over the years, the nut has gone under several names: the Romans called *Juglans regia* the "Persian nut" because they obtained supplies from Persia. The English dubbed it walnut (from Old English *walh-hnuta*, meaning "foreign nut"), probably because they obtained the nuts from Gaul. Americans originally called it "English" walnut—not that it came from England but because the Persian nuts were shipped on English sailing vessels.

Most food historians believe the walnut originated in ancient Persia, passing along trade routes to Greece, Italy, Spain, India, China and Japan. The ancient peoples would grind walnuts either to make into a paste to thicken sauces, stews and sweet dishes, or to use as a powdered spice to flavor food. The Greeks pressed them for oil; the Romans thought them a great delicacy and the perfect ending to a meal to eat with fruit.

The nut was also used as a hair coloring and for dyeing wool, as well as for various medicinal purposes. For example, ancient Romans thought the two corrugated halves of a walnut resembled the two hemispheres of the human brain, and believed the nut cured headaches; later in the Middle Ages, the French believed walnuts *caused* headaches.

When the Franciscan fathers from Spain and Mexico established the chain of Californian missions in the eighteenth century, they planted walnut trees in the mission courtyards and surrounding gardens, never knowing that a couple of hundred years later walnuts would be grown in California on a huge commercial scale (400 million pounds annually).

Zucchini Walnut Bread

By summer's end, gardeners often have an overabundance of zucchini, and worry they'll never find enough ways to use all the extra squash. But happily, this is a versatile vegetable, and it's easy to turn an excess into a delicious opportunity. This quick-bread is packed with plump meaty raisins and the fall's harvest of nuts.

1½ cups unbleached all-purpose flour
½ teaspoon *each* baking powder and baking soda
½ teaspoon *each* salt and ground cinnamon
½ cup granulated sugar
½ cup light brown sugar
2 large eggs
½ cup (1 stick) melted butter or soy margarine
1 teaspoon vanilla extract
1 cup unpeeled, coarsely grated zucchini squash
½ cup *each* dark raisins and chopped walnuts

Position rack in center of oven, preheat oven to 350 degrees F., and lightly grease a 9 x 5 x 3" loaf pan.

In a 2½ quart mixing bowl, sift flour, baking powder, baking soda, salt, cinnamon and granulated sugar. Add brown sugar. Stir to blend thoroughly and make a well in center.

In a 1½ quart bowl whisk eggs with butter, vanilla extract and grated zucchini. Stir into flour mixture just until flour is moistened. Gently fold in raisins and walnuts. Spoon into prepared loaf pan.

Bake at 350 degrees F. for about 1 hour, or until a test toothpick inserted in center comes out clean. Cool loaf for 15 minutes in pan before removing to a wire rack.

Makes one 9 x 5 x 3" loaf, about 14 slices.

Each slice contains about: 218 calories, 3g protein, 30g carbohydrate, 1g fiber, 10g fat, 48mg cholesterol, 197mg sodium.

Chapter 5

Savory Specials

You may think of muffins as essentially sweet, but a savory style can bring out the special qualities of fresh produce; other vegetable ingredients can be stock items from your freezer or pantry shelf. Sauté raw vegetables in a tiny spoonful of oil to soften them; or use a cup or half-cup of cooked vegetables leftover from a previous meal—too good to waste; instead of throwing out, throw them in the batter.

Give muffins a new twist with the appeal of fresh garden herbs, epicurean mustards and other gourmet condiments, flavored oils and vinegars. Remember to crush dried herbs such as thyme and rosemary in the palm of your hand to release the peak of flavor before adding to muffin mixtures.

Try small amounts of zesty, sharp aged natural cheeses (a good way to utilize those last scraps and awkward pieces), either grated and stirred into the muffin batter or used as a light sprinkling on top that bakes to an appetizing golden crust.

How to Enjoy an Artichoke

This sharp-thorned giant thistle might intimidate you if you haven't bought or tackled one before; here's a simple guide about getting to know this delicate-tasting vegetable.

How to buy: Artichokes are mature when picked. Look for compact heads that are plump and seem heavy for their size. They should be a fresh green color—not looking tired, dusty or wilted. Although available practically year-round, during colder weather markets often sell artichokes with brown or whitish areas on the outer leaves, but that's not a problem.

How to prepare: With a sharp knife, cut off stems from medium-size or larger artichokes, to make them stand upright, and about a quarter of the tops. Break off and discard the outer ring of leaves from the bottom, and with sharp scissors snip off the thorns from the leaf tips. Wash in plenty of cold water and drain well.

How to cook: Place artichokes upright in a large saucepan with 2 inches of water and 2 tablespoons mild vinegar or lemon juice. Cover pan securely with lid, bring pan to a boil and simmer gently for between 25 and 45 minutes, depending on size of 'chokes. When done, a center leaf should pull out easily. Remove with a slotted spoon and drain upside down.

How to serve: Artichokes make a delicious first course, either hot with mayonnaise or melted butter, or cold with a vinaigrette dressing or a few drops of olive oil. You can eat them as a side vegetable with the main entrée, or have a large 'choke as the star item on the menu.

How to eat: Serve each artichoke on a large plate, together with a small individual bowl of dipping sauce, cold mayonnaise or melted butter. Pull off each leaf, starting at the bottom, and dip the fleshy base into the sauce. Put the base of the leaf between your teeth and scrape off the fleshy pulp; leave the inedible remainder of the leaf on your plate. Continue, one leaf at a time, down to the inedible center leaves. Using a fork or spoon, remove the fuzzy 'choke part, to reveal the heart or artichoke bottom. Cut the heart in small chunks, dipping each in the sauce. Divine!

Artichoke Parmesan Bread

This savory bread is good served warm from the oven with an herbed fresh tomato soup, a tossed salad with Italian dressing, or with a bowl of pasta as an alternative to garlic bread.

1 (6-oz) jar marinated artichoke hearts
1 tablespoon cooking oil
2 cups unbleached all-purpose flour
2 teaspoons baking powder
2 tablespoons granulated sugar
½ teaspoon *each* salt and garlic powder
¼ teaspoon baking soda
1 large egg
¼ cup cooking oil
1 cup nonfat skim milk
1 tablespoon lemon juice
3 tablespoons grated Parmesan cheese

Drain artichoke hearts and chop coarsely. Discard marinade (or use as a salad dressing). In a small pan gently sauté artichoke pieces in cooking oil until softened but not brown, stirring three or four times. Remove from heat; cool to room temperature.

Position rack in center of oven, preheat oven to 400 degrees F. and lightly coat an 8" or 9" square shallow pan with nonstick cooking spray.

In a 2½ quart mixing bowl, sift flour, baking powder, sugar, salt, garlic powder and baking soda. Stir to blend and make well in center.

In a 1½ quart bowl whisk egg, oil, milk and lemon juice. Beat thoroughly, then add to flour mixture, stirring just until flour is moistened. Fold in artichokes to distribute evenly. Spoon batter into prepared pan. Sprinkle top evenly with Parmesan cheese, and gently pat it into batter.

Bake at 400 degrees F. for 25 minutes. Cool slightly in pan. While still warm cut into squares and serve immediately.

Makes 12 squares, about 2" x 3".

Each square contains about: 170 calories, 4.5g protein, 20g carbohydrate, 1.5g fiber, 8g fat, 19mg cholesterol, 281mg sodium.

Capers: Beads of Flavor

Romans and Greeks were well acquainted with capers since ancient times, probably obtaining their supplies from species that grew in the Sahara and adjoining regions. In the tenth century at a banquet given by Caliph Mustakfi in Baghdad, a guest Ibn al-Mu'tazz described a tray of appetizers:

Here capers grace a sauce vermilion
Whose fragrant odors to the soul are blown.

What are they? Capers are the immature unopened flower buds of the caper bush *Capparis spinosa* which grows wild in arid areas, from Mediterranean Europe to northwestern India, and is cultivated on sunny terraces mainly in Spain, France and Italy. The flower buds on the spiny bramble-like shrub have a sharp, piquant taste. When the buds are young and tender, the workers pluck them daily in early morning, and later pickle them in vinegar. (If not picked as buds, the flowers go on to become caper *berries, taprots* in Spanish, which can be pickled too; they look like big striped grapes and taste like a cross between capers and pickled okra.)

Capers vary considerably in size, but are generally like small peas, depending on the variety and stage of development when picked. Connoisseurs prefer the smallest capers (*nonpareil* variety), but flavor is determined more by processing than by size.

Because of the hand labor involved in picking, and because most are imported (only a small quantity is grown in Florida and California), capers tend to be expensive, but you need just small quantities of the *picante* little beads to make flavorful dishes and sauces that otherwise would be bland and insipid. As an economy, large capers can be chopped. Try a few capers in rice casseroles, egg dishes and in cole slaw.

Most capers are pickled in vinegar and sold in small jars; they keep for months in the original bottle in the refrigerator. Before using, drain off liquid.

Caper Picante Muffins

Serve these savory muffins with scrambled eggs or a steaming bowl of split-pea soup for a satisfying supper.

1⅞ cups unbleached all-purpose flour
1 teaspoon *each* baking powder and onion powder (not onion salt)
½ teaspoon *each* baking soda, salt and ground black pepper
2 tablespoons granulated sugar
1 large egg
1 cup nonfat skim milk
1 tablespoon lemon juice
¼ cup (½ stick) melted butter or soy margarine
½ cup *nonpareil* capers, drained
1 teaspoon paprika pepper

Position rack in center of oven, preheat oven to 400 degrees F., and lightly coat muffin wells with nonstick cooking spray.

In a 2½ quart mixing bowl, sift the first seven dry ingredients. Stir to blend and make a well in center.

In a 1½ quart bowl whisk egg, milk, lemon juice and melted butter. Beat thoroughly. Add to flour mixture, stirring only until flour is moistened. Gently fold in capers. Spoon batter into prepared muffin wells. Dust tops with paprika.

Bake at 400 degrees F. for 20 to 25 minutes or until done. Cool in pan 5 minutes before turning out onto wire rack.

Makes about 12 2½" muffins.

Each muffin contains about: 142 calories, 3.5g protein, 22g carbohydrate, 1g fiber, 4.5g fat, 28mg cholesterol, 278mg sodium.

Mustard: Spread It Around

Americans eat more mustard than anyone else in the world—at least ten 4-oz jars (915 grams) per person per year—way ahead of the French, Germans, Swedes and British. But there's far more to the condiment than the mild-flavored, technicolor-yellow spread used lavishly by many Americans. Import shops, specialty food stores and well-stocked super-markets offer dozens of mustard varieties, so you can choose from a whole world of new ones, whether imports from great mustard centers as Dijon and Dusseldorf (which alone has 1,500 varieties!) or their U.S.-made equivalents.

There's a surging interest in mustards of various strengths and flavors: from mild to bold to explosively hot; from mellow to intensely spiced; from palest yellow to dark brown; from velvety smooth to coarsely ground husky seeds.

What goes into mustard? As well as black, brown or white mustard seed and water, mixtures can include:

Wine, wine vinegar and verjuice (sour-grape juice): In many styles. Wineries create mustards with white wine or red, using Cabernet, Chardonnay or Zinfandel and other grapes. (Mustard, from Latin *mustum*, "new wine," was first made by mixing *only* grape juice with mustard powder.)

Beer: "Real ale" mustards use some of Britain's best brews.

Salt and flour: Imported British mustard may have flour, said to absorb the natural oils of the mustard seed.

Sugar and honey: Bavarian and Scandinavian mustards are often sweetened with sugar; the British styles with honey.

Spices: Turmeric is used to boost the natural yellow color of mustard seed. Other spices used are chilies, black and green peppercorns, allspice, fennel seeds and jalapeño peppers!

Herbs: The classic mustard herb is tarragon, used in many French, German and American mustards. British mustard makers add chives, thyme and horseradish. Scandinavian and American companies add dill.

Whiskey: Famous distillers make whiskey mustards.

Other flavors: Creole style; Chinese style—powerfully hot; Hawaiian style—sweet hot with pineapples and honey; British, with cider or cider vinegar; and blends with mayonnaise.

Cheddar Mustard Muffins

The tang of fresh Cheddar is accentuated by English mustard to add zest to these muffins. They are good with bowls of French onion soup for a quick supper in winter, or served alongside a chilled plate of salad greens for a light summer luncheon.

1¼ cups sour milk
1 cup whole bran
1½ cups unbleached all-purpose flour
2 tablespoons granulated sugar
1½ teaspoons baking powder
1 teaspoon dry English mustard
½ teaspoon salt
¼ teaspoon baking soda
1 large egg
¼ cup (½ stick) melted butter or soy margarine
1 cup grated sharp Cheddar cheese

In a 1½ quart bowl pour sour milk over bran to soften. Set aside about 10 minutes.

Position rack in center of oven, preheat oven to 400 degrees F., and lightly coat muffin wells with nonstick cooking spray.

In a 2½ quart mixing bowl, sift flour, sugar, baking powder, mustard, salt and baking soda. Stir to blend and make well in center.

Whisk egg into milk/bran mixture, gradually adding melted butter. Beat thoroughly. Add to flour mixture, stirring just until flour is moistened. Do not overbeat. Stir in grated Cheddar. Spoon into prepared muffin wells.

Bake at 400 degrees F. for 25 to 30 minutes. Turn onto wire rack to cool slightly. Serve warm.

Makes about 12 2½" muffins.

Each muffin contains about: 163 calories, 6g protein, 19g carbohydrate, 2g fiber, 8g fat, 38mg cholesterol, 263mg sodium.

Corn: A Cultural Heritage

In Mexico, corn (maize) is more than just a food item—it's a cultural heritage with deep symbolism. Mexicans call themselves "the children of corn," descendants of people whose religious pantheon included three corn gods. Cornstalks were common patterns in ancient Mexican art; clay statues of Aztec hairless dogs (A.D. 200 to 800) held corncobs in their mouths. Even today, people use corn in sacred ceremonies and herbal cures; corn pollen and husk-figures are part of religious rites and holiday celebrations; Mexicans toss corn kernels to read fortunes from them like tea leaves.

Archeologists estimate that wild corn discovered in caves in Puebla in Central Mexico is 7,000 years old—the most ancient evidence of human corn consumption. In the caves of Tehuacán near Mexico City, wild corn dates back to 5200 B.C., and humans have been cultivating corn since about 3400 B.C.

Mexico grows at least thirty-two varieties of corn and devotes two-thirds of the fields to native maize varieties. More than 600 corn dishes are at the heart of Mexican cuisine, and the differences in corn varieties play a large role in the diversity of regional recipes. Everything is made from corn (but not from the same *type* of corn): hot spicy soups (*pozole*), triangular corn puffs (*cornudos*) and thick hot drinks (*atole*); corn silk is brewed to make a diuretic tea; cornmush with a filling is steamed inside cornhusks (*tamales*); and every neighborhood has its *tortilleria* where the women line up to buy tortillas by the kilo.

Thrifty farmers use every part of the corn plant: cobs and stalks are fed to animals, burned as fuel, or woven into roofing material.

Although times change in Mexico, dress and hairstyles are modern, and only the oldest villagers still speak an Indian language, the traditions and ceremonies connected with corn are among the few obvious remnants of their traditional culture. The people continue to plant native corn in the ways of their ancestors.

Corn Sage Muffins

Perfect partners with hearty bowls of vegetable chili and a tossed green salad, these muffins have the pleasantly gritty texture of corn, sparked with sage for a touch of the southwest.

1 cup unbleached all-purpose flour
3 tablespoons granulated sugar
3 teaspoons baking powder
½ teaspoon salt
1 teaspoon crushed dried sage
¾ cup coarse yellow cornmeal
1 large egg
1 cup nonfat skim milk
¼ cup (½ stick) melted butter or soy margarine
½ cup canned corn kernels, well drained

Line muffin wells with paper cases or lightly coat with nonstick cooking spray.

In a 2½ quart mixing bowl, sift flour, sugar, baking powder and salt. Stir in sage and cornmeal to blend, then make well in center.

In a 1½ quart bowl whisk egg, milk and melted butter. Beat thoroughly. Add to flour mixture and stir just until flour is moistened. Stir in corn kernels until well distributed. Do not beat. Spoon into prepared muffin wells.

Bake in a preheated oven at 400 degrees F. for 20 to 25 minutes, until golden brown and a test toothpick inserted in centers comes out clean. Turn out onto wire rack.

Makes about 12 2½" muffins.

Each muffin contains about: 133 calories, 3g protein, 20g carbo-hydrate, 1g fiber, 4.5g fat, 28mg cholesterol, 252mg sodium.

Garlic: Rose of Gilroy

The "Garlic Capital of the World" is generally considered to be the Gilroy area of California which produces 200 million pounds of garlic every year, giving the valley a marvelous aroma, especially during its annual Garlic Festival in July. Although sometimes referred to as the "stinking rose," garlic is a member of the lily family, *Allium sativum.*

Garlic has had a prominent place in folklore and medicine since ancient history, and has always had a certain mystique. The first written record of garlic is found in Sanscrit writings around 5000 B.C. The ancient Egyptians had a great love of the pungent bulb, and it is said that the builders of the pyramids wouldn't work without their daily garlic rations. Several cloves of garlic were discovered in Tutankhamen's tomb, probably as a talisman to ward off evil spirits and disease in the After Life. Garlic was planted in the gardens of the King of Babylon, and praised in the writings of Homer.

Greeks and Romans prescribed garlic for many ailments and to promote good health: warriors and gladiators took garlic prior to battle to ensure strength and courage, necklaces of garlic cloves were said to ward off personal devils, and garlic rubbed on doorknobs and window-frames discouraged vampires. The Crusaders introduced garlic to Europe when they returned from the Holy Land; but they weren't all in favor of it, as in 1330 King Alfonso XI of Castile organized an order of knights based solely on a *distaste* of garlic.

Old herbalists prescribed garlic as prevention or cure for countless ailments in folk medicine, from acne to nervous disorders to the plague. Early Egyptians used garlic in a test for infertility, and Muhammad recommended garlic as a balm to soothe scorpion stings. To fight infection, the British used it in World War I, the Russians in World War II. Even today, chewing garlic is supposed to relieve toothache; rubbing a cut clove over and around the ear is said to cure earache; it is claimed that garlic can help reduce blood pressure and lower blood cholesterol; and the Japanese have found that garlic is helpful in treating stomach ulcers. There's no doubt that garlic stimulates the palate and can be used as a salt substitute.

Garlic Cheese Appetizers

A tray of these appetizers disappears fast—you may want to make a double recipe. They freeze well, if tightly wrapped, so you can prepare them ahead of time when planning a party.

4 medium garlic cloves
1 tablespoon light olive oil
2 cups unbleached all-purpose flour
2 tablespoons granulated sugar
2 teaspoons baking powder
½ teaspoon salt
¼ teaspoon *each* baking soda and ground black pepper
2 large eggs
¾ cup nonfat skim milk
3 tablespoons light olive oil
1 tablespoon mild vinegar
2 to 4 tablespoons grated sharp Cheddar cheese

Position rack in center of oven, preheat oven to 400 degrees F., and lightly grease a 9" square shallow pan.

Mince garlic cloves and sauté with olive oil in a small saucepan until just softened. Set aside.

In a 2½ quart mixing bowl, sift flour, sugar, baking powder, salt, baking soda and black pepper. Stir to blend and make a well in center.

In a 1½ quart bowl whisk eggs, milk, olive oil and vinegar. Beat thoroughly. Add to flour mixture and stir until flour is just moistened. Gently fold in garlic until well distributed. Spoon and spread batter into prepared pan.

Bake at 400 degrees F. for 15 minutes. Sprinkle lightly cooked batter with cheese and return to oven for 10 more minutes. Cool slightly in pan; serve warm. Cut into squares.

Makes about 16 2" appetizers.

Each appetizer contains about: 111 calories, 3g protein, 15g carbohydrate, .5g fiber, 4.5g fat, 28mg cholesterol, 140mg sodium.

A User's Guide to Garlic

What to buy: Look for large, plump bulbs that are white and firm—not stained, spongy or shriveled. Elephant garlic is extra large but it is mild-flavored. Larger markets sell bottled garlic cloves marinated in oil. Garlic powder and garlic salt are convenient when fresh garlic supplies are low.

When to buy: Bulbs are available year-round. Major crops are June through December from California; January from Argentina; February to May from Mexico; and March from Chile.

Where to store: Keep garlic in a well-ventilated cool, dry place—not the refrigerator. Store them in a paper sack, not plastic which will turn bulbs brown. Many kitchen supply stores sell garlic "cellars," usually pottery jars with perforations. Another method: store peeled garlic cloves covered with olive oil in a screw-top glass jar in the refrigerator.

How to peel: Place clove on cutting board and whack with the flat side of a wide knife; pull broken skin away. For several cloves, drop them in boiling water for 15 seconds; rinse with cold water, drain, and remove skin.

How to mince: Peel clove, place on chopping board. Slice into pieces, then chop finely. Crushing, mincing or finely chopping garlic releases pungent juices, making it more potent than when halved, sliced or left whole.

How to determine flavor: If left raw, garlic is pungent, assertive and robust. When lightly cooked, it becomes mellow and sweet. When cooked longer and slower, and allowed to caramelize, the flavor becomes more delicate, nutty and rich. Don't let it become too brown or burnt as it will turn bitter.

How to remove odor: Rub a cut lemon over fingers and chopping board, then rinse under cold running water.

How to remove garlic breath: Yeast-based capsules (sold by Bon Monjay of Davis, CA) are being test-marketed, and these reduce the gases that cause garlic breath. Alternatively, buy odor-free garlic (processed by Jewel Rina of Yorktown, VA). The bulbs are doused in a silica solution which removes offensively-smelling breath but not the flavor and aroma in cooking (however, current prices are breathtaking).

Garlic Onion Muffins

These robust-flavored muffins go well with hearty soups and salads, or as a snack with a cup of vegetable broth. The small-sized muffins make perfect nibbles for a buffet table when you have a few friends over for the evening.

3 garlic cloves, finely minced
1 tablespoon melted butter or soy margarine
2 cups unbleached all-purpose flour
1 tablespoon baking powder
1 teaspoon salt
2 tablespoons granulated sugar
1 large egg
½ cup cooking oil
¾ cup nonfat skim milk
2 tablespoons finely chopped green onion tops
4 oz cream cheese, diced

Lightly grease muffin wells or coat with nonstick cooking spray.

Sauté garlic in butter until tender; set aside. In a 2½ quart mixing bowl, sift flour, baking powder, salt and sugar. Stir to blend and make a well in center.

In a 1½ quart bowl whisk egg, oil and milk. Beat thoroughly. Add to flour mixture and stir just until flour is moistened. Fold in garlic, chopped onion and diced cream cheese until evenly distributed. Spoon into prepared muffin wells.

Bake in a preheated oven at 400 degrees F. for 20 minutes. (Bake mini muffins about 15 minutes.) Cool 5 minutes in pans before removing to wire rack.

Makes about 18 to 24 mini muffins or 12 2½" muffins.

Each mini muffin contains about: 146 calories, 2.5g protein, 13g carbohydrate, .5g fiber, 9g fat, 21mg cholesterol, 207mg sodium.

Chili: 'Raising the Dead'

To the horticulturist, chilies are fruits; to the botanist, they are berries; to supermarket managers, fresh chilies are vegetables and dried chilies are spices. But from Mexico to Thailand, from Africa to Indonesia, the chili is *the* spice of life.

Wild chilies probably originated in the Andes of present-day Bolivia and, with birds dispersing the seeds, eventually spread across Central and South America. At Tehuacán, southeast of Mexico City, the archeological record shows that wild chili was eaten in Mesoamerica as far back as 7000 B.C., and domesticated by 2500 B.C. Chilies—from mild to wildly hot—were added to nearly every dish, whether corn, potatoes or meat; and Montezuma, the last of the Aztec rulers, relished a daily drink of hot chilies and chocolate. But chilies weren't just eaten—they were worshipped by Mayans and Aztecs.

When Columbus arrived in the New World searching for black pepper and other precious spices of Asia, he found chilies and named them "peppers," mistakenly thinking they were related to *Piper nigrum* (the berry that is ground to make black and white pepper), which they are not. Chilies *(capsicums)* are part of the nightshade *(Solanaceae)* family, which includes tomatoes, eggplants and potatoes.

Columbus brought chilies back to the Old World where they spread like wildfire! Within a century, chilies had blazed along trade routes and into the spicy cuisines of all continents—especially India, Asia and Africa. In doing so, they adapted to different climates, environments and culture, so that today chilies splash innumerable flamboyant colors on the culinary scene: some are green, red or yellow; some are violet, brown, white or orange. Some are bulbous, oval or heart-shaped; others are long and tapered, conical or cylindrical. They can vary in size from foot-long down to pea-size. Flavor can be extremely mild and sweet, ranging to hellishly hot when a mere touch on the tongue is painful. Strangely enough, the larger the chili, the milder the flavor—usually. The tiniest chilies pack the most fire, earning names such as "gringo killer" or "raising the dead," when the taste buds of even ardent chili-lovers beg for mercy.

Green Chili Texas Bread

Vary the voltage of the chili to suit your taste: leave the seeds intact for full impact (if your taste buds are fire-resistant), or remove them to temper the heat.

2 tablespoons butter or soy margarine
2 canned Ortega chilies
1 cup unbleached all-purpose flour
¾ cup cornmeal
¼ cup granulated sugar
2 teaspoons baking powder
½ teaspoon salt
1 large egg
1 cup nonfat skim milk
⅓ cup grated sharp Cheddar cheese

Lightly coat an 8" square shallow pan with nonstick cooking spray.

In a small saucepan heat butter. Chop green chilies and sauté till softened. Set aside to cool.

In a 2½ quart mixing bowl, sift flour, cornmeal, sugar, baking powder and salt. Stir to blend and make a well in center.

In a 1½ quart bowl whisk egg, milk and cooled chilies. Stir mixture into dry ingredients until flour is just moistened. Fold in grated cheese. Pour into prepared pan.

Bake in a preheated oven at 425 degrees F. for about 20 minutes until golden brown. Cut into 12 squares and serve warm.

Makes 12 squares, about 2 x 2½".

Each square contains about: 126 calories, 4g protein, 19g carbohydrate, 1g fiber, 4g fat, 26mg cholesterol, 234mg sodium.

Herb Chart

Herbs can be combined for specific foods, to enhance your reputation as a gourmet. Here's a guide to show what goes with what:

Basil: Tomato soup, vegetable soup, chowders, aspic, Russian dressing, squash, cauliflower, tomatoes, waffles and croutons.

Bay leaves: Onion soup, tomato aspic, French dressing, in cooking water with potatoes, carrots and tomatoes.

Cayenne: Bean salads, French dressing, asparagus, broccoli, eggplant, gravies.

Celery seed: Celery soup, lentil soup, cole slaw, cauliflower, okra, asparagus, rolls and biscuits.

Chili powder: Chowders, pepper pot soup, kidney bean salad, Mexican corn, baked beans, gravies and croutons.

Curry: Sour cream dressings, cooked vegetables, cooked rice, waffles and rolls.

Dill seed: Split-pea soup, sour-cream dressing, cabbage, cauliflower, sauerkraut.

Garlic powder: Vegetable soup, green and vegetable salads, potato salad, eggs, tomatoes and garlic breads.

Marjoram: Onion soup, spinach soup, tomato aspic, herb dressings, carrots, mushrooms, spinach, herb breads and cornbread.

Mint: Cottage cheese salad, green peas, chocolate cake.

Oregano: Tomato soup, minestrone, vegetable salads, Italian dressing, tomatoes, cabbage, broccoli, herb breads, croutons.

Paprika: Creamed soups, garnishes, cole slaw, French dressing, baked potatoes, onions, cauliflower, rolls.

Poppy seed: Rice, asparagus, cottage cheese, turnips, cakes, cookies, breads and dumplings.

Rosemary: Vegetable soups, tomato aspic, herb dressing, most vegetables, cornbread and biscuits.

Sage: Consommés, chowders, herb dressings, French dressing, brussels sprouts, lima beans, eggplant.

Thyme: Chowders, herb salad dressing, broccoli, brussels sprouts, mushrooms, herb breads.

Herbed Cottage Muffins

This is a versatile recipe: vary the herbs to harmonize with the other dishes on your menu. See Herb Chart on opposite page.

1½ cups unbleached all-purpose flour
2 tablespoons granulated sugar
2 teaspoons baking powder
½ teaspoon salt
¼ teaspoon baking soda
1 tablespoon finely chopped chives
1 teaspoon ground marjoram
2 large eggs
¼ cup (½ stick) melted butter or soy margarine
½ cup nonfat skim milk
½ cup small curd (4% fat) cottage cheese
½ cup shredded zucchini, lightly spooned into cup

Position rack in center of oven, preheat oven to 400 degrees F., and lightly grease muffin wells.

In a 2½ quart mixing bowl, sift flour, sugar, baking powder, salt and baking soda. Add chives and marjoram. Stir to blend and make a well in center.

In a 1½ quart bowl whisk egg, melted butter, milk and cheese. Beat thoroughly. Add to flour mixture, stirring just until flour is moistened. Gently fold in zucchini. Spoon into prepared muffin wells.

Bake at 400 degrees F. for 25 to 30 minutes, until golden brown. Remove from pan to wire rack to cool slightly. Serve warm.

Makes about 12 2½" muffins.

Each muffin contains about: 125 calories, 4g protein, 15g carbohydrate, .5g fiber, 5g fat, 47mg cholesterol, 251mg sodium.

Leeks: Pride of Wales

Although little known and rarely used in the United States, leeks with their distinctive fragrance have been popular and cultivated all over Europe and China for centuries.

The long-shaped bulb belongs to the onion family, but where leeks originated seems to be the subject of some discussion. They were cultivated by ancient peoples around the Mediterranean, and Juvenal wrote that Egypt was a country where "onions are adored and leeks are gods." According to Herodotus, leeks were among the rations of the workers who built the pyramids; and Cheops paid his court magician a fee which included 100 bunches of leeks.

They were evidently valued not only as a vegetable but also for their medicinal qualities: an Assyrian herbal recommended leeks to keep the hair from turning gray; Hippocrates taught that leeks prevented nose-bleed; Nero was said to eat leek soup daily to improve his voice; and more recent folk medicine suggests that leek syrup can help calm coughing and even whooping cough.

Leeks are particularly identified with the British Isles, where wild leeks grow freely in hedgerows and especially on the offshore islands of Wales. On St. David's Day, Welshmen are proud to tuck bits of leek in their buttonholes and hat-bands, as the national emblem of Wales; this custom is to commemorate victory over the Saxons in A.D. 640 when the Welsh had worn leeks in their caps as distinctive badges in battle. They were thus able to identify and recognize each other and avoid striking the wrong fighters.

When shopping for leeks, look for fresh green tops and white unstained bulbs. One large bunch generally serves about four people. Trim leeks, leaving about 1½ inches of the green tops. Grit between bulb layers can be tiresome; be sure to wash leeks thoroughly in plenty of cold water before cooking. Serve leeks piping hot with a little melted butter, or slip the cooked stalks under the broiler in a fireproof dish with a sprinkling of salt, pepper, thyme and grated cheese.

Leek Cheese Bread

The grated cheese melts and toasts on top to make a golden brown quick-bread with a tantalizing savory aroma. Serve warm, to accompany a southwest-style salad of beans, chopped jicama, hard-cooked egg and green onion tossed with a ranch dressing.

1 tablespoon vegetable oil
1½ cups finely chopped leeks (2 medium)
2 cups unbleached all-purpose flour
2 teaspoons baking powder
½ teaspoon salt
¼ teaspoon baking soda
2 tablespoons granulated sugar
1 large egg
¼ cup (½ stick) melted butter or soy margarine
1 cup nonfat plain yogurt
½ cup nonfat skim milk
½ cup grated sharp Cheddar cheese

Heat oil in a small pan and sauté leeks until softened but not brown, about 10 minutes, stirring three or four times. Remove from heat and let cool to room temperature.

Position rack in center of oven, preheat oven to 400 degrees F., and lightly coat a 9" square pan with nonstick cooking spray.

In a 2½ quart mixing bowl, sift flour, baking powder, salt, baking soda and sugar. Stir to blend and make a well in center.

In a 1½ quart bowl whisk egg, butter, yogurt and milk. Beat thoroughly. Add to flour mixture, and stir just until flour is moistened. Gently fold in leeks to distribute evenly. Spoon into prepared pan.

Bake at 400 degrees F. for 15 minutes. Sprinkle partly cooked batter with cheese and return to oven for 10 more minutes. Cool slightly in pan; serve warm. Cut into squares.

Makes nine 3" squares.

Each square contains about: 234 calories, 7g protein, 29g carbo hydrate, 1g fiber, 9.5g fat, 45mg cholesterol, 342mg sodium.

Mushrooms: Pick of the Crop

The best plan is to do your foraging in the market, as picking wild mushrooms is hazardous for the amateur. Poisonous mushrooms can cause serious illness and even death; antidotes don't exist for many poisonous varieties. Mushrooms in supermarkets are, of course, safe and the selection is usually wide; here are some of the most common:

Chanterelle: Golden yellow, almost flowerlike. Sometimes black or white. Fruity, peppery flavor. Available fresh, dried and canned.

Enoki: A somewhat bizarre shape: a tiny button on a long, thin stem. Delicate texture and flavor. Use raw in salads, or add at last minute to stir-fries. Available fresh. A Japanese delicacy.

Italian brown (also called **Crimini**): Light brown cap. Very flavorful. Grill, broil, stuff, or add to stews, soups and sauces. Available fresh.

Morel: Range in color from light tan to dark brown or black with long conical caps with wrinkles. Both caps and stems are hollow and edible (but if morel is large, stem can be tough). Slightly nutty, earthy flavor. One of the finest fungi. Available fresh, dried and canned.

Oyster: Pearl gray cap, softly ruffled. Delicate flavor. Best raw in salads with a lemon vinaigrette or cooked briefly. Available fresh or dried.

Porcini: Brown cap on long stem. Distinctively earthy, rich and almost meaty flavor. A robust mushroom for sauces, stews and soups. Available fresh and dried.

Shiitake: (also called **Black Forest** or **Golden Oak**): Broad cap, tough stems. Spongy texture. Flavor: woodsy, peppery, smoky, and almost meaty. Sauté caps lightly with garlic, as appetizers. Available fresh and dried.

Straw: Small brown mushrooms from the Orient. Soft texture, mild flavor. Attractive in stir-fries. Only available canned.

White button: Very smooth white cap. Mild flavor. Good raw, baked and sautéed, or tossed in soups and stews. Widely available fresh and canned.

Wood ear (also called **Tree ear**): Dark Oriental mushroom. Mild flavor. Good texture to add to soups and stir-fries. Available fresh and dried.

Mushroom Muffins

Simple but elegant muffins that can add a gracious touch to the most sophisticated dinner menu for your discriminating guests.

3 oz fresh shiitake mushrooms
1 tablespoon light olive oil
1⅞ cups unbleached all-purpose flour
2 tablespoons granulated sugar
2 teaspoons baking powder
½ teaspoon salt
¼ teaspoon *each* ground black pepper and ground nutmeg
1 large egg
1 cup nonfat skim milk
¼ cup (½ stick) melted butter or soy margarine
½ teaspoon Hungarian ground paprika

Line muffin wells with paper cases or lightly coat with nonstick cooking spray.

Coarsely chop mushrooms and sauté in oil for 5 minutes. Set aside to cool.

In a 2½ quart mixing bowl, sift flour, sugar, baking powder, salt, nutmeg and pepper. Stir to blend and make a well in center.

In a 1½ quart bowl whisk egg, milk and butter; beat thoroughly. Add to flour mixture and stir only until flour is moistened. Gently fold in mushrooms to distribute evenly. Spoon batter into prepared muffin wells. Dust tops with paprika.

Bake in a preheated oven at 400 degrees F. for about 20 to 25 minutes, or until a test toothpick inserted in centers comes out clean. Cool in pan 5 minutes then turn onto wire rack.

Makes about 12 2½" muffins.

Each muffin contains about: 140 calories, 3.5g protein, 19g carbohydrate, .5g fiber, 5.5g fat, 28mg cholesterol, 199mg sodium.

Onions: Weep No More

During the Civil War, General Ulysses S. Grant sent a message to the War Department: "I will not move my Army without onions." He got them, without question, because armies had always traveled with onions: originally they were supposed to make men courageous in battle and later, more to the point, they made dull Army rations more palatable. But did the troops weep in the kitchen?

Cooking can be a joy, but peeling, slicing and chopping onions can be a pain, bringing tears to novice and pro alike. How can this be?

We prize onions for the pungency and special flavor they give to foods, but those esteemed volatile oils contain much sulfur. When you peel an onion, an enzyme called *allinase* bonds with sulfur in the onion as soon as it is exposed to the air; the release of fumes from the oils irritates the tear ducts, mixing with the moisture in your eyes to make what amounts to a mild sulfuric acid. Fresh onions can be particularly vicious.

Cooks go to extraordinary lengths to avoid tears; an informal survey of friends has turned up some wild attempts to stave off sobbing: peeling onions under running water (*that* makes onions soggy); or clamping a piece of apple, a crust of bread or a toothpick between the teeth, or a clothes-pin on the nose, so that breathing is through the mouth. Others wear scuba gear, ski-goggles or a gas-mask! Some insist the stem-end should be cut first, or cut lengthwise first rather than widthwise—even believing that such procedure gives a better flavor!

The best solution? Simply *chill* the onions before chopping. Store bulk supplies of onions in a mesh-type bag and hang it somewhere airy, dry and cool—not in a root cellar where onions might go bad. Then, for day to day needs, keep a supply in the refrigerator where the chilling completely subdues the fumes, but has no effect on flavor and texture. Never peel onions when they are at room temperature: chill them in the refrigerator at least two hours, or in the freezer for five to ten minutes, before peeling and slicing. Presto! no more crying!

Onion Poppy Seed Cornbread

A robust-flavored quick-bread, with its attractive baked-on savory topping, that will be a favorite for family suppers.

¼ cup (½ stick) butter or soy margarine
¾ cup finely chopped onion
1 cup unbleached all-purpose flour
3 teaspoons baking powder
½ teaspoon salt
2 tablespoons granulated sugar
1 cup coarse yellow cornmeal
2 large eggs
1 cup nonfat skim milk
4 tablespoons *each* mayonnaise and grated Parmesan cheese
2 teaspoons poppy seeds

Lightly grease an 8" square shallow pan.

In a small saucepan melt butter and sauté ½ cup of the onion for about 5 minutes or until softened. Remove from heat and set aside to cool.

In a 2½ quart mixing bowl, sift flour, baking powder, salt and sugar. Stir in cornmeal to blend thoroughly, and make a well in center.

In a 1½ quart bowl whisk eggs and milk; beat thoroughly. Add to flour mixture and stir just until flour is moistened. Gently fold in sautéed onion, and stir until evenly distributed. Spoon batter into prepared pan.

In a 1½ pint bowl blend mayonnaise, Parmesan and remaining ¼ cup onion, and beat until light. Spread evenly over top of batter. Sprinkle top with poppy seeds.

Bake in a preheated oven at 350 degrees F. for about 35 minutes, until the top is puffed and browned, and a test toothpick inserted in center comes out clean. Cut into 9 pieces.

Makes nine squares, about 2½" square.

Each square contains about: 248 calories, 6.5g protein, 27g carbohydrate, 2g fiber, 13g fat, 67mg cholesterol, 400mg sodium.

Chilies:
Some Are Hot, Some Are Not

Here's a "temperature guide" to help you shop for fresh or dried chilies (capsicums) usually found in U.S. markets:

Anaheim (also called **California Green** or **Ortega**): About 5 inches long, 1½ inches diameter. Fresh ones are bright shiny green; canned are soft and a moss green. Flavor: ranging from mild like a bell pepper to fairly hot.

Ancho: Appearance similar to bell pepper, but more peppery flavor and firmer texture. When dried, it becomes wrinkled like a prune; color may range from dark red to almost black.

Bell peppers: About 4 inches long, 3 inches diameter; bright shiny green, and new hybrids of yellow and red. Flavor: mild and sweet, especially red.

Cayenne: A powder ground from small red to yellow chilies. Very hot, to be used with caution.

Chili powder: A blend of ground dried chilies; sometimes includes cumin and oregano. Hot and fragrant.

Chiltepin: The smallest dried round chilies, the size of peas. Picked from wild plants in Mexico. Red color. One of the hottest.

Fresno: Conical shape, 2 inches long, 1 inch diameter. Bright green changing to orange and then red at maturity. Hotter than Anaheim, ranging from mildly hot to painful. Often sold pickled.

Habañero: Small and innocuous-looking, but reputed to be the hottest chili in the world, probably originating near Havana, Cuba.

Hontaka and **sontaka:** Small tapered chilies about 1 inch long, imported from Japan. Often found in pickling-spice mixtures.

Jalapeño: About 2½ inches long, 1 inch diameter. Dark green. Very hot. Often sold canned or pickled.

Paprika: The powder ground from mild sweet chilies. Gourmets consider the best powder is imported from Hungary.

Pasilla: About 7 to 12 inches long, 1 inch diameter. Dark green when immature, ripening to dark brown. Dried form: chocolate-brown. Mild to peppery hot.

Pimiento: Usually sold in jars or cans, in strips or pieces. Soft flesh; mild sweet flavor, similar to red bell pepper.

Serrano: About 1 to 1½ inches long, ½ inch diameter. Extremely hot. When fresh: a rich, waxy green, changing to orange then red when mature. Often sold canned, pickled or packed in oil.

Pimiento Herb Muffins

In spite of their fiery red color, pimientos are one of the mildest and sweetest chilies, here accented by thyme to make a bright tasting muffin. Pimientos may be replaced by one-half cup chopped red pepper sautéed in one tablespoon butter.

1 jar (2 oz) sliced pimientos
1⅞ cups unbleached all-purpose flour
2 tablespoons granulated sugar
2 teaspoons baking powder
1½ teaspoons ground chili powder
½ teaspoon salt
¼ teaspoon freshly ground black pepper
1½ teaspoons ground thyme
1 large egg
1 cup nonfat skim milk
¼ cup (½ stick) melted butter or soy margarine

Lightly grease muffin wells, or line with paper cases. Drain pimientos and chop finely; set aside.

In a 2½ quart mixing bowl, sift flour, sugar, baking powder, chili powder, salt and black pepper. Stir in thyme to blend and make a well in center.

In a 1½ quart bowl whisk egg, milk and butter; beat thoroughly. Add to flour mixture, stirring only until flour is moistened. Gently fold in chopped pimientos until evenly distributed. Spoon batter into prepared muffin wells.

Bake in a preheated oven at 400 degrees F. for about 20 minutes, or until a test toothpick inserted in centers comes out clean. Cool in pan 5 minutes then turn onto wire rack.

Makes about 12 2½" muffins.

Each muffin contains about: 129 calories, 3.5g protein, 19g carbohydrate, .5g fiber, 4.5g fat, 28mg cholesterol, 200mg sodium.

Rosemary: 'Dew of the Sea'

Rosemary (in the Mint family) is one of the most romantic of herbs—at least the Romans thought so, since the Latin name *rosmarinus* means "dew of the sea" originating from the wild rosemary growing luxuriantly on the islands of Corsica and Sardinia. Pliny wrote that the herb grew best in dewy places, and rosemary always thrived where fogs rolled in from the sea, wafting fragrance far out across the ocean.

Rosemary was much used in religious ceremonies, for weddings, funerals and church holy days; so when the name was later anglicized, *rosmarinus* became rose-*mary* to honor the Virgin. According to Sir Thomas More, it was a symbol of fidelity for lovers and of life everlasting, a herb "sacred to remembrance, to love, and to friendship." Centuries earlier, the Egyptians had put bunches of rosemary in their tombs, the ancient Romans placed sprays of rosemary in the hands of their dead. Even today rosemary is often a fragrant component of funeral wreaths.

Ancient herbalists believed rosemary had many fine qualities and practical uses, including "strengthening the memory," stimulating the brain, uplifting the spirits and rekindling energy. Branches placed under the pillow would be a powerful charm against witchcraft and the "evil eye," warding off not only bad dreams but also black magic and wicked spells during the night. The burned and crushed stems made an old-time toothpowder, and prevented baldness; rosemary tea was an old stomach and headache remedy; the leaves boiled in rainwater made a facial rinse for milady's flawless complexion and a hair rinse to condition her long tresses.

In Tudor times it was the custom to plant rosemary close to footpaths, to scent ladies' swirling skirts and gentlemen's capes as they brushed against it. In the home, rosemary sprigs tied with colorful ribbons were placed between linens, in closets and around bookcases, not only to provide a lovely fragrance but also a deterrent to moths. Rosemary was sewn into herbal pillows, sweet sachets, and included in potpourris.

Rosemary Buttermilk Muffins

The texture of these beauties is somewhere between biscuits and muffins. They're superb for a family supper with steaming bowls of black-bean soup, or for a leisurely weekend breakfast served with home-style country gravy.

Since rosemary is a pungent herb, small amounts give best results—too much, and you introduce bitterness. It teams well with many other spices, and makes a delicious addition to batters of quick-breads and muffins, as well as the cooking liquid of vegetables such as eggplant, cauliflower, green beans, beets, summer squash and turnips.

2 cups unbleached all-purpose flour
2 tablespoons granulated sugar
4 teaspoons baking powder
½ teaspoon *each* salt, baking soda and onion powder
1 teaspoon dried rosemary
½ cup vegetable shortening, melted
1 cup buttermilk
2 tablespoons freshly grated Parmesan cheese

Position rack in center of oven, preheat oven to 400 degrees F., and line muffin wells with paper cases.

In a 2½ quart mixing bowl sift flour, sugar, baking powder, salt, baking soda and onion powder. Add crushed rosemary; stir to blend and make a well in center.

In a 1½ quart bowl whisk melted shortening with buttermilk; beat thoroughly. Add to flour mixture, stirring only until flour is moistened. Spoon into prepared muffin wells. Sprinkle tops with cheese.

Bake at 400 degrees F. for 15 minutes or until golden brown. Cool slightly for 5 minutes in pan before turning onto wire rack. Serve warm.

Makes about 12 2½" muffins.

Each muffin contains about: 174 calories, 3g protein, 19g carbohydrate, .5g fiber, 9g fat, 2mg cholesterol, 274mg sodium.

Olive Oil: Flavor of Spain

The Andalusian countryside in Spain is dotted with olive trees, and stacks of barrels at the pressing cooperatives. Spain is currently the world's largest producer and exporter of olives and olive oil, and about 90 percent of the annual crop is crushed for oil. Olives have to be processed in some way or another before using, to remove the natural bitterness: green olives, picked unripe, are processed with a potassium or ash solution, pickled in brine, then left to age a few months. The plump and fleshy *manzanilla* is probably the most popular table olive, and the one most often stuffed.

Fruits to be pressed for oil are left on the trees until they mature. Oil olives, such as the small Mission variety grown in California, are often harvested over several months. Mature green fruit harvested in early fall produces an oil that is typically green color with a slightly sharp flavor. Riper fruit picked during the winter months yields oil that is usually golden, fruitier, smoother and more velvety in flavor. Producers generally press oil from several pickings of fruit throughout a season, let it age, and then blend. About ten pounds of olives are needed for one quart of oil.

The International Olive Oil Council in Madrid defines the grades for olive oil: the first pressing, cream of the crop, is *extra virgin* (the best flavors and the highest price). Next come *virgin, pure* (a blend) and *refined* (which has undergone a heat process to make it neutral in color, flavor and aroma). Olive oils labeled *light* have the same number of calories as any other olive oil, but are refined to give mildness.

A well-stocked market will offer a dozen or more olive oils, with prices varying from about $3 to ten times that amount, and colors ranging from clear and pale, to gold, to pale green.

The wide selection can be confusing; which oil is best? Try this: dip a chunk of plain bread into the oil and taste. For salads and seasoning vegetables, extra virgin olive oil works well; but for cooking, extra virgin is extravagant as heat lessens its flavor and it's apt to smoke at moderate temperatures. Sauté with a pure or refined olive oil.

Stuffed-Olive Appetizers

Baking with olive oil is common in Mediterranean countries, where a number of traditional Italian, Greek and Spanish cake recipes use it. Spread slices of this quick-bread with cream cheese, and serve as attractive party hors d'oeuvres. Best baked the day before you need them, for easy slicing.

⅔ cup (3 oz jar) pimiento-stuffed manzanilla olives
2 cups unbleached all-purpose flour
2 tablespoons granulated sugar
2 teaspoons baking powder
1 teaspoon onion powder (not onion salt)
½ teaspoon salt
¼ teaspoon *each* baking soda and ground black pepper
2 large eggs
¾ cup nonfat skim milk
¼ cup light olive oil
1 tablespoon mild vinegar
Cream cheese (optional)

Position rack in center of oven, preheat oven to 350 degrees F. and lightly grease a 9 x 5 x 3" loaf pan.

Drain olives, slice thinly and set aside.

In a 2½ quart mixing bowl, sift together dry ingredients. Stir to blend and make a well in center.

In a 1½ quart bowl whisk eggs, milk, olive oil and vinegar; beat thoroughly. Add to flour mixture, stirring just until flour is moistened. Gently fold in chopped olives until well distributed. Spoon batter into prepared loaf pan.

Bake at 350 degrees F. for 50 minutes to 1 hour, or until a test toothpick inserted in center comes out clean. Cool in pan for 15 minutes then turn out onto wire rack. Slice evenly, and spread with cream cheese.

Makes one 9 x 5 x 3" loaf, about 14 slices. If more convenient, batter may be made into mini-muffins: bake at 400 degrees F. for about 15 minutes or until done.

Each slice (excluding cream cheese) contains about: 133 calories, 3g protein, 17g carbohydrate, .5g fiber, 6g fat, 30mg cholesterol, 267mg sodium.

Tomatoes: 'Apples of Gold'

The tomato originated on the slopes of the lower Andes, in Ecuador, Peru and Bolivia, in South America, from weedy plants bearing berries the size of currants or cherries, in green, orange or red. The tomato wasn't a cultivated food of the Incas; pre-Columbian Peruvians merely gathered the wild fruit in season. But by the time of the Spanish Conquest, the cherry tomato had been domesticated and was eaten in Mexico, and the Mexicans gave the plant its common name, derived from the Nahuatl word *tomatl*.

When the first tomato seeds were taken across the Atlantic to Europe, they were small yellow-fruited varieties; the original Peruvian tomato of the sixteenth century was the *pomo d'oro,* translated as "apple of gold." The fruit probably first went to Spain, and then quickly on to Italy via the kingdom of Naples which in 1522 was ruled by the Spanish. The Italian word *pomodoro* appears to have been corrupted by the French to *pomme d'amour,* meaning "love apple," as the fruit had the reputation of being an aphrodisiac.

Opinions were divided about the fruit: while the Italians showed real enthusiasm for using the tomato in cooking, elsewhere in Europe the people resisted it and viewed it with suspicion, believing it to be toxic or having adverse health effects. Although established in England by the end of the sixteenth century, it was only as an ornamental plant, and it remained so for 200 years. The idea persisted that the fruit was poisonous—perhaps because the foliage really is. Some people even thought that eating a raw tomato was suicidal: a cookbook in 1860, *Godey's Lady's Book,* cautiously suggests that tomatoes should "always be cooked for three hours"—in hopes perhaps the tomato's "poison" would be neutralized!

Only in the twentieth century was the tomato finally accepted as edible, and indeed highly esteemed for the healthy goodness packed beneath the skin. Shop at farmers' markets for organically-grown vine-ripened fruit from heirloom varieties of seeds, and then indeed you can recapture the truer old-fashioned flavor of tomatoes worthy of the name "apples of gold."

Tomato Corn Squares

When winter comes and you long for the sunny taste of red-ripe summer tomatoes, the pale offerings in markets seem tasteless and disappointing; but you can depend on canned tomato products as convenient standbys at any time of the year to add wonderfully concentrated flavor to soups and casseroles. Each square of this quick-bread is suffused with the rosy red of tomato sauce and the subtle flavor of herbs. Serve the squares warm with hot vegetable soup on a cold wintry day.

1 medium size tomato (firm)
1 cup unbleached all-purpose flour
2 tablespoons granulated sugar
2 teaspoons baking powder
¼ teaspoon *each* baking soda, salt, black pepper and
    ground oregano
¾ cup dry polenta cornmeal
1 large egg
½ cup *each* nonfat skim milk and seasoned canned tomato
    sauce
¼ cup (½ stick) melted butter or soy margarine

Position rack in center of oven, preheat oven to 400 degrees F., and lightly grease an 8" square shallow pan.

Chop tomato finely (should make ½ cup) and set aside.

In a 2½ quart mixing bowl, sift flour, sugar, baking powder, baking soda, salt, pepper and oregano; add cornmeal. Stir to blend and make a well in center.

In a 1½ quart bowl whisk egg till foamy, add milk, tomato sauce and melted butter. Beat thoroughly. Add to flour mixture and stir only till flour is moistened. Gently stir in chopped tomato. Spoon into prepared pan.

Bake at 400 degrees F. for 25 minutes, or until a test toothpick inserted in center comes out clean. Cut into squares and serve warm.

Makes 12 squares 2" x 2½".

Each square contains about: 123 calories, 3g protein, 18g carbohydrate, 1.5g fiber, 5g fat, 28mg cholesterol, 231mg sodium.

Chapter 6

'Ultralites'

When juggling with diets and striving to keep weight within limits, are rich-tasting muffins an impossible extravagance? The critical question is: Are they really such a great indulgence? Remember that indulging doesn't have to mean *over*indulging, and few diets are harmed by occasional luxury.

But times have changed. Food fashion and health concerns have turned our buttery-rich world upside down; lean cuisine is stylish; and fancy menus at famous weight-reducing spas across the country lack one key ingredient—fat.

Fat takes up about 40 percent or more of the average American's meals each day, even though nutritionists, doctors and government agencies have been urging us for some time to cut that amount to 30 percent or less.

We do need fatty acids in our diet—but not as much as most of us eat. And while some people prudently change to more healthful vegetable oils such as olive oil and canola oil, when it comes to calories, fat is fat, and all varieties have about the same large number per given measure. (A daily diet of about 2,100 total calories needs less than 70 grams of fat daily; with 1,500 total calories, the fat count should be less than 50 grams daily. So although the muffins and quick-breads in preceding chapters are already low in fat, in this chapter they are ultra low—"ultralite."

Dieters rejoice! If your goal is to trim fat, "ultralites" may well fit into your food plan and become more than a rare treat. By cutting the maximum of sinful fat from a recipe, you can still enjoy luscious home-baked muffins and quick-breads, and indulge yourself more often than special occasions—guilt-free!

Ask any cooks worth their salt if delicious muffins can be baked with so little fat and they will say "Impossible! Can't be done!" Yet the recipes in this chapter prove that "lean" baking can be successful, satisfying, and setting new standards of cooking. Here is old-fashioned flavor using a revolutionary new style—a cooking secret your mother could never have told you.

These innovative recipes are unbelievably rich, moist and flavorful, yet low in fat and calories; the fat has been pruned to the bone by using natural fat substitutes. The amazing thing is that if you didn't know you were eating lowfat muffins, you'd probably never guess.

What's the role of fat in baking?

Traditional baking of muffins, quick-breads and cakes has always meant using fat not only to deliver taste and texture but also to keep breads more moist and fresh for a longer time. Butter and shortening make baked products moist because they cannot evaporate. Enter fat substitutes.

What's in a fake-fat?

Because many of us dream of desserts that combine self-indulgence and self-control, food manufacturers across the country have been spurred to find ingenious ways to invent and develop fake-fats. The push was on in all directions and food manufacturers have responded by formulating a myriad of fake-fats and synthetics in answer to our demands. The current buzz words splashed across packages are "lite," "fat free," "low-calorie" and "cholesterol free." In the 1990s they launched 1,200 new reduced-fat bakery products, and the major aim of research and development among food processors continues to be fat reduction.

But here's the rub: you'll find that when commercial bakers reduce fat in their recipes or switch to imitations, the ingredient description on the label becomes longer with chemicals you can't understand. Frequently, synthetic fats are high-tech, engineered foods including the strange addition of starches and gums that try to mimic the taste, texture and "mouthfeel" of fat. Imagine eating a so-called lowfat muffin containing xanthan gum, dicalcium phosphate, diglycerides and vegetable protein. Who needs all these? It's chemistry—not cuisine!

Many of the new lowfat low-calorie baked goods in supermarkets depend on artificial additives that are questionable; some fake-fats are still being reviewed by the Food and Drug

Administration and have yet to receive FDA approval, while others that have succeeded in being officially approved feel strangely odd in your mouth or leave a peculiar after-taste that makes them undesirable. Even Oliver Twist would have been repelled.

Although research clearly shows benefits from eating less fat than the average American diet and maintaining a desirable weight, there's no sure evidence that eating fake-fats leads automatically to better health or weight loss. Artificial food synthetics don't replace sound nutrition.

So what's the alternative? *Natural* fat substitutes.

What's in a natural fat substitute?

Along with the familiar baking ingredients in this chapter (such as flour, milk, salt, baking powder and so on), you'll find wholesome alternatives in a selection of purées from apples, apricots, pears, prunes and other fruits, plus fruit butters, apple sauce and cottage cheese, to replace butter and other fat. You "prune" and "pear" the fat!—simply, naturally and effectively. (Completely fat-free isn't worth it, but a gram or two can work wonders.)

How much can you save?

Using fruit purées and fruit butters trims fat by *75 to 90 percent*, calories by *20 to 30 percent*, and cholesterol to *zero*. The big plus is the flavor is fantastic, the moistness is marvelous, the slight chewiness is mouth-satisfying, and the keeping quality of the quick-breads is enhanced. You may find "ultralites" are even better a day or so after baking.

Not only that: fruit purées come naturally packed with dietary fiber, vitamins and minerals—which neatly ties in with the prodding from health authorities that we should eat more daily servings of fruit.

Purées, fruit 'butters' and baby-food

For a concentrated fruit taste, make purée from dried fruit that has a pliable squeezable texture rather than the rock-hard kind of dried fruit (see recipes on page 180).

For a less intense fruit flavor, instead of dried fruit you can purée fresh produce: fruits that are high in natural pectins such as tart apples, crabapples, cranberries, currants, gooseberries, loganberries, plums and quinces. Commercial applesauce is a good short-cut. Supermarkets are beginning to sell containers of pre-measured, ready-to-bake applesauce and prune purée in the baking section of the stores.

Another time saver is to buy ready-made commercial fruit "butters" such as apple butter, plum butter and plum purée (lekvar), to shorten preparation and use immediately in recipes. If your local stores don't stock them at present, make your own (see recipe on page 182) or purchase them by mail order (see Appendix 3).

To further downplay the flavor of the fruit, jars of baby-food fruit purées work well because the taste is more bland, although their consistency is apt to be a little thin. Check the jar labels as some of them are not 100 percent fruit and may contain a proportion of tapioca.

How much do you use?

As a general guideline, one-half cup fruit purée, or two 2½-ounce jars of baby-food purée, can replace one-half cup butter, margarine, oil or shortening in a recipe.

How do purées work?

Researchers are still puzzling out exactly how fruit purées act as fat substitutes; the answer seems to be that nearly half the fiber in prunes, for instance, is *pectin;* and these pectins help to form a "film" around air in batters, similar to the way butter and shortening work, giving them volume, "lift" and lightness. In addition, fruits contain natural *sorbitol* (a mildly sweet sugar-alcohol), technically called a "humectant" to attract and bind moisture, that makes muffins tender and keeps them fresh-tasting for a longer time, with the "mouthfeel" usually found in fat-laden baked goods.

Pectins in fruit also trap and enhance natural flavors in each recipe: for instance, prunes can bring out the flavor of chocolate, coffee, vanilla and cinnamon; apple and pear purées accentuate the flavor of spices such as lemon, cloves and ginger; apricot purée enhances almond flavoring.

The end result is lean or lowfat muffin-making far superior to any products from store or bakery. You *can* have your diet and eat fabulous tasting muffins too. You've simply got to try this new-era baking for yourself to find out how good it really is!

Further tips on 'Ultralite' baking

Other ways to cut fat and cholesterol include substituting two egg whites for every whole egg (*saving:* 5 grams of fat); for strict diets, use egg substitute; use skim milk, buttermilk or nonfat yogurt in place of whole (4% fat) milk (*saving:* about 8 grams of fat per cup); and spraying muffin wells and baking pans with nonstick cooking spray instead of grease. Note: using paper cases for "ultralite" baking is not recommended since the paper can stick obstinately to each muffin and spoil your pleasure.

You'll also notice that these "ultralites" specify a small increase in baking soda to adjust for the acidity derived from the various fruits. Baking time should take a little longer, at a reduced oven temperature, compared to regular muffins using butter or shortening. The resulting muffins are usually somewhat darker in color than those from full-fat recipes, and the texture will generally be more moist and chewy. After trying a few recipes, you may prefer to reduce the amount of sugar according to taste, to adjust for the natural sugars present in the fruit.

When lowfat muffins taste this good, you'll probably decide to make a permanent switch to "ultralite" cooking, and bake no other way! This new-style baking doesn't have to be limited to muffins and quick-breads: try homemade purées as wholesome fat substitutes in your favorite recipes for cakes and brownies. And as for that all-important raw-batter taste test—you'll have a bowl really worth licking!

Classic Applesauce

Commercial ready-made applesauce is a handy convenience for lowfat "ultralite" baking; yet home-made applesauce takes only minutes to prepare, you can leave it slightly chunky or silky smooth according to your preference, and include various spices or a splash or two of lemon juice for a distinctive tartness. Ask your produce manager for the best cooking apples as improved varieties are constantly being developed. Learn to know and appreciate your local varieties. Bland-flavored or sweet dessert apples do not make good applesauce.

Basic method

2 lbs. (6 to 8) cooking apples
½ cup water
Few grains of salt
½ cup granulated sugar (or up to 1 cup,
    depending on type of apple and
    sweetness desired)

Wash, core and quarter apples (but do not peel). Put apples in pan and cook slowly until soft. Stir occasionally to prevent sticking and scorching. Put through a coarse strainer to remove skins and seeds. Add salt. Add sugar to taste, and stir until sugar dissolves completely. Add spices, such as cinnamon or cloves, and lemon juice if apples need more flavor or tartness.

Makes about 1 quart.

Pressure cooker method

Cook apples for 5 minutes with ¼ cup water. Strain and add sugar according to basic recipe.

Microwave oven method

Put apples and water in a 3-quart glass dish. Cover with plastic wrap, vented. Cook 10 minutes on HIGH. Stir once. Strain and add sugar according to basic recipe.

Applesauce Lites

These home-baked treats, deliciously moist with applesauce, bake to a rich dark brown; they make a wholesome snack for any time of the day.

½ cup *each* applesauce *(in place of ½ cup butter)* and
  buttermilk
½ cup *each* bran cereal shreds and light brown sugar,
  packed
2 tablespoons vegetable oil
Whites only from 3 large eggs
1 cup unbleached all-purpose flour
1½ teaspoons baking soda
½ teaspoon ground cloves
¼ teaspoon salt
1 teaspoon grated orange peel
2 tablespoons raw oatmeal

Position rack in center of oven, preheat oven to 375 degrees F., and coat muffin wells with nonstick cooking spray.

In a 2½ quart mixing bowl stir together applesauce, buttermilk, bran cereal, brown sugar and oil. Set aside 10 minutes to soften. Whisk egg whites until foamy and stir into cereal mixture.

In a 1½ quart bowl sift together flour, baking soda, cloves and salt. Add orange peel and stir to blend. Add flour mixture to cereal mixture and stir just until flour is moistened. Gently fold in oatmeal until evenly distributed. Spoon batter into prepared muffin wells.

Bake at 375 degrees F. for 25 minutes, or until a test toothpick inserted in centers comes out clean. Cool in pan 15 minutes. Turn onto wire rack to cool completely.

Makes about 12 2½" muffins.

*Each muffin contains about: 117 calories, 3g protein, 22g carbohydrate, 1.5g fiber, **2.5g fat**, 0 cholesterol, 215mg sodium.*

Fruit Purée: Give It a Whirl

New-style baking that replaces butter or shortening with fruit purée makes a dramatic difference to the calorie-count and grams of fat put into muffins and quick-breads. With ¾ cup butter containing about 1,219 calories and 138 grams of fat, compare these numbers with the following purées:

Apricot purée

1 cup dried apricots
6 tablespoons hot water
1 teaspoon vanilla extract
Makes ¾ cup apricot purée,
   with 253 calories, .5g fat

Peach purée

1 cup dried peaches
6 tablespoons hot water
1 teaspoon vanilla extract
Makes ¾ cup peach purée,
   with 314 calories, .8g fat

Cranberry purée

1 cup dried cranberries
   (craisins)
3 tablespoons hot water
1 teaspoon vanilla extract
Makes¾cup cranberry purée,
   with 484 calories, 1.8g fat

Prune purée

1⅓ cups dried pitted
   prunes
6 tablespoons hot water
1 teaspoon vanilla extract
Makes 1 cup prune purée,
   with 344 calories, .5g fat

Date purée

1 cup pitted dates
6 tablespoons hot water
1 teaspoon vanilla extract
Makes ¾ cup date purée,
   with 366 calories, .7g fat

Raisin purée

1 cup seedless raisins
3 tablespoons hot water
1 teaspoon vanilla extract
Makes¾cup raisin purée,
   with 314 calories, .2g fat

Basic method

Combine fruit, water and vanilla extract in container of food processor. Pulse on and off until fruit is finely chopped. Cool before use.

Apricot Almond Lites

Choose California dried apricots for their more intense flavor and rich dark color.

1¾ cups unbleached all-purpose flour
2 teaspoons baking powder
½ teaspoon baking soda
¼ teaspoon salt
⅓ cup granulated sugar
Whites only from 2 large eggs
¾ cup nonfat skim milk
2 tablespoons vegetable oil
½ teaspoon almond extract
¾ cup apricot purée (opposite page) or apricot butter

Position rack in center of oven, preheat oven to 400 degrees F. and lightly coat muffin wells with nonstick cooking spray.

In a 2½ quart mixing bowl sift flour, baking powder, baking soda, salt and sugar. Stir to blend and make a well in center.

In a 1½ quart bowl whisk egg whites until foamy. Add milk, oil, almond extract and apricot purée (or apricot butter). Beat thoroughly. Add to flour mixture and stir just until flour is moistened. Spoon into prepared muffin wells.

Bake at 400 degrees F. for about 20 minutes, or until a test toothpick comes out clean. Allow to cool in pan 15 minutes before turning onto wire rack.

Makes about 12 2½" muffins.

*Each muffin contains about: 162 calories, 4g protein, 32g carbohydrate, 2g fiber, **2.5g fat**, 0 cholesterol, 153mg sodium.*

Apple Butter

Old-fashioned apple butter is very simple to prepare. You can also make butters with fruits such as fresh apricots, cranberries, peaches, plums, or whatever pulp is left in the jelly bag after making jelly. Short of time? Commercial apple butters are difficult to find in stores, but you can buy the spread by mail order (see Appendix 3). For more about "butters" without fat, turn to page 186.

> 16 medium-size apples (about 6lbs) (Jonathan, McIntosh,
>   Winesap or other well-flavored cooking varieties)
> 2 quarts water
> 1½ quarts apple cider
> 1½ lbs granulated sugar
> 1 teaspoon *each* ground allspice, ground cinnamon and ground
>   cloves

Wash, core and cut the apples into small pieces (should be about 4 quarts). Cover with water in a large saucepan and boil until soft. Mash pulp with a potato masher then put through a sieve to remove skins and seeds.

Bring cider to boiling and add apple pulp and sugar. Cook until mixture thickens, stirring frequently to prevent sticking and scorching. Stir in spices and cook until apple butter is thick enough for spreading.

A traditional test for doneness is to dab a spoonful of apple butter on a plate and turn the plate upside down. The butter should be thick enough to stick to the inverted dish.

Pour into sterilized jars and seal. Makes about 4 pints.

Alternative oven method

After adding cider and sugar to pulp, bake it in a large covered casserole at 300 degrees F. for about 2 to 2½ hours. Stir every 15 minutes until butter is thick but not dry.

Banana Oatmeal Lite-Loaf

A rich golden brown, with the tropical flavor of banana. Serve with iced tea, or hot tea with lemon slices.

¼ cup apple butter *(in place of ¼ cup melted butter)*
2 large bananas, well-mashed
Whites only from 4 large eggs, well beaten
1 teaspoon vanilla extract
2 cups unbleached all-purpose flour
¾ cup granulated sugar
1 teaspoon salt
1½ teaspoons baking soda
½ cup raw oatmeal

Position rack in center of oven, preheat oven to 350 degrees F. and coat a 9 x 5 x 3" loaf pan with nonstick cooking spray.

In a 2½ quart mixing bowl whisk bananas, egg whites and vanilla. Beat thoroughly. Lightly stir in flour, sugar, salt and baking soda. Add oatmeal and mix gently but thoroughly to blend. Spoon into prepared loaf pan.

Bake at 350 degrees F. for 45 minutes, then at 325 degrees F. for 15 minutes, or until a test toothpick inserted in center comes out clean. Cover with foil the last 15 minutes if necessary, to prevent overbrowning. Cool in pan 15 minutes before turning out onto wire rack. When cool, wrap well and serve, preferably the following day for easy slicing.

Makes one 9 x 5 x 3" loaf, about 14 slices.

Each slice contains about: 148 calories, 3.5g protein, 33g carbohydrate, 1g fiber, .5g fat, 0 cholesterol, 257mg sodium.

A User's Guide to Chocolate

Storage

Baking chocolate: Store at room temperature. During the summer you can refrigerate it because it contains no sugar and won't develop "sugar bloom."

Chocolate (bittersweet, milk or semi-sweet): Keep in a cool, dry place where the temperature stays about 70 degrees F. During hot weather, refrigerate it; it might "bloom" when you bring it to room temperature. "Sugar bloom" occurs when condensation forms on the surface of semi-sweet or milk chocolate, causing sugar to dissolve and rise to the surface. "Cocoa butter bloom" is the gray discoloration caused when chocolate is stored above 78 degrees; the chocolate melts and cocoa butter rises to the surface. Bloom looks unattractive, but flavor is unaffected.

Chocolate flavored syrup: After opening, store in the refrigerator.

Cocoa, cocoa mix and instant chocolate powder: Keep in tightly sealed containers at room temperature.

Substitutions

1 oz, one square, baking chocolate or one envelope pre-melted unsweetened chocolate	=	3 tbsp cocoa + 1 tbsp oil OR 3 tbsp carob powder + 2 tbsp water.
6 oz semi-sweet chocolate	=	6 tbsp cocoa + ¼ cup cooking oil + 7 tbsp sugar.
4 oz bar sweet cooking chocolate	=	3 tbsp cocoa + 2⅔ tbsp cooking oil + 4½ tbsp sugar.
1 oz cocoa powder	=	1 oz carob powder

Mix cocoa (and sugar) with the dry ingredients; add the extra oil to the shortening called for in recipe. Don't use butter or margarine when making these substitutions because they contain a small amount of water which could separate ingredients.

Choco-Lites

Loaded with rich dark chocolate, these wonderfully moist aromatic muffins taste like a million calories. With this much flavor and tenderness, who would guess that the wicked fat has been pruned dramatically and cholesterol is zero? A dieter's dream!

1 cup plus 2 tablespoons unbleached all-purpose flour
¾ cup granulated sugar
¾ cup unsweetened cocoa powder
1½ teaspoons baking powder
½ teaspoon baking soda
¼ teaspoon salt
Whites only from 3 large eggs
1½ teaspoons vanilla extract
½ cup prune purée (see page 180) *(in place of ½ cup shortening)*
¾ cup water

Position rack in center of oven, preheat oven to 350 degrees F., and coat muffin wells with nonstick cooking spray.

In a 2½ quart mixing bowl, sift the first six ingredients. Stir to blend and make a well in center.

In a 1½ quart bowl, whisk egg whites with vanilla extract, prune purée and water. Add to flour mixture. Stir just until blended. Spoon into prepared muffin wells.

Bake at 350 degrees F. for 25 minutes or until a test toothpick comes out clean. Leave to cool on wire rack for 15 minutes before removing from pan.

Makes about 12 2½" muffins.

*Each muffin contains about: 132 calories, 3g protein, 30g carbohydrate, 3g fiber, **1g fat**, 0 cholesterol, 173mg sodium.*

'Butters' Without Fat

When early settlers came to this country, while the men of the household labored in the fields or tended livestock, the women worked in the dairy, then took the butter, cream, cheese and eggs to market to earn much-needed cash. For spreads on their home-baked breads, they turned to the trees around the homestead to make surplus fruit into "butters," the most common being apple butter, since apple trees were the ones most often planted by the colonists.

Many interesting tales are handed down from the *schnitzing* (apple slicing) days of long ago. Phebe E. Gibbons in *The Pennsylvania Dutch* writes:

"Two large copper kettles were hung under the beech-trees down between the springhouse and smoke-house, and the cider was boiled down the evening before, great stumps of trees being in demand...the rest of the family gathered in the kitchen and labored diligently in preparing the cut apples."

The evening before the apple butter was to be made, young folks in the neighborhood would come in to help pare the apples. Between chatter, sweet cider and popcorn, the required bushel and a half of apple *schnitz* was soon prepared. After the butter was cooked in the huge kettles, and the last crock was filled, gifts of butter would be handed to each neighbor as they departed.

With the urbanization of America, these old-time recipes for fruit butters were lost, forgotten or went out of fashion. But a revival of these spreads is now underway, on a wave of nostalgia and with a search for new and better ways to replace or reduce fats in our diet, giving a surge in popularity for butters made from many kinds of fruit, including pumpkin.

A fruit butter is nothing more than fruit, a small amount of brown or white sugar or sometimes honey, and some spices or maybe lemon. Basically the butter is made by long cooking over very low heat until it becomes a thick smooth concentrate. Not as sweet as jam or jelly, and at only 10 calories per teaspoon, you can afford to slather it on muffins, pancakes, or over a scoop of cottage cheese.

Cranberry Spice De-Lites

The tart-sweet taste of cranberries is beautifully accented by the spices in these reduced-calorie muffins.

1 ⅞ cups unbleached all-purpose flour
2 teaspoons baking powder
1 teaspoon baking soda
¼ teaspoon ground cloves
2 tablespoons granulated sugar
1 large egg
1 cup nonfat skim milk
⅓ cup cranberry purée (see page 180) *(in place of ⅓ cup vegetable oil)*
1 tablespoon lemon juice
½ cup fresh cranberries (or frozen, thawed), finely chopped

Position rack in center of oven, preheat oven to 375 degrees F., and coat muffin wells with nonstick cooking spray.

In a 2½ quart mixing bowl sift flour, baking powder, baking soda, cloves and sugar. Stir to blend and make a well in center.

In a 1½ quart bowl whisk egg with milk, fruit purée and lemon juice. Beat thoroughly. Add to flour mixture and stir just until blended. Carefully fold cranberries into batter. Spoon into prepared muffin wells.

Bake at 375 degrees F. for about 25 minutes. Allow muffins to rest in pan for 10 minutes before cooling on a wire rack.

Makes about 12 2½" muffins.

*Each muffin contains about: 113 calories, 5g protein, 23g carbohydrate, 1g fiber, **1g fat**, 18mg cholesterol, 139mg sodium.*

A User's Guide to Ginger

Fresh ginger. In the produce section of supermarkets and health-food stores, generally shipped from Hawaii. The rhizome (tuberlike stem) should be hard with a tan-colored smooth skin—not wrinkled, which would show that it's beyond prime condition. Do not remove skin until ready to use. (Spring ginger has a thin pale skin that doesn't need peeling.) Wrap root tightly in plastic, store in refrigerator, and use within two weeks. When grated, it adds a fresh zip to muffins, quick-breads and cakes. When minced (easily done in food processor or blender), it brings intriguing flavors to stir-fried dishes and dipping sauces.

Cooked stem ginger in syrup. In the gourmet foods section of the supermarket or in specialty food stores, imported from China or Australia. Pieces of peeled ginger stem are simmered in sugar syrup then sold in glass jars or decorative stoneware. Preserved stem ginger can be diced to use in baking quick-breads, sliced thinly as an elegant sandwich filling on whole-wheat bread, or slivered and tossed over ice cream.

Cooked crystallized ginger. In the baking products section or candy department of the supermarket. Slices or cubes of stem ginger are cooked in sugar syrup, dried, then coated with granulated sugar. Can be chopped and used in baking, frostings and fillings, or eaten as candy. Check the level of sweetness; you may want to reduce the amount of sugar in a baking recipe.

Ground ginger. In the baking products section of the supermarket, usually imported from India and China; some of the best comes from the island of Jamaica. The fresher the spice, the hotter it is. Use ground ginger in gingerbread, gingersnaps, cookies, pancakes, pies and spice cakes.

Dehydrated ginger (instant ginger). A new product. When liquid is added, the ginger expands ten-fold, to resemble fresh ginger purée in appearance, taste and texture. Use similar to fresh ginger.

Ginger Lite-Bread

This lightly-styled gingerbread, low in fat and calories, will become a favorite. It's easy to assemble and bake, making a delicious dessert for family supper.

1 cup molasses
½ cup apple butter *(in place of ½ cup melted butter)*
½ cup buttermilk
Whites of 2 large eggs, well beaten
2 cups unbleached all-purpose flour
1½ teaspoons *each* baking soda and ground ginger
¼ teaspoon ground cloves
½ teaspoon salt
½ cup dark raisins

Position rack in center of oven, preheat oven to 325 degrees F., and coat an 8" square pan with nonstick cooking spray.

In a saucepan heat together molasses and apple butter; allow to cool. Add buttermilk and beaten egg whites.

In a 1½ quart bowl sift flour, baking soda, ginger, cloves and salt. Stir to blend. Add to molasses/buttermilk mixture. Fold in raisins to distribute evenly. Spoon into prepared pan.

Bake at 325 degrees F. for 35 to 40 minutes, or until test toothpick comes out clean. Cut into squares. Serve warm.

Makes 16 2" squares.

Each square contains about: 138 calories, 2.5g protein, 32g carbohydrate, 1g fiber, .25g fat, 0 cholesterol, 163mg sodium.

Lemons: Zest for Life

In ancient Rome, lemons were always rare and expensive, but by the eighth and ninth centuries the Moors were cultivating them in the Sahara and had established lemon orchards in Andalusia, Spain, and later Sicily. Even then, only the very rich could afford them.

Herbalists and early cookbook writers believed lemons and their juice had many medicinal benefits and were prescribing them for all kinds of uses: an antidote for poison, a diuretic, a tonic for teeth and gums, a remedy for respiratory ailments and bad breath, relieving a fever, hiccups, pimples, sunburn and so on; and the ladies of King Louis XIV's court would bite into lemons from time to time to make their lips pleasingly pink.

Using lemons and other citrus has been much-chronicled in connection with the prevention of scurvy that afflicted sailors on long voyages when they were deprived of fresh fruits and vegetables. In 1601, when the English East India Company dispatched its first ships to the East, a ship's log recorded that the little fleet stopped off the island of Madagascar to gather "oranges and lemons of which we made good store of juice, which is the best remedy against scurvy." After 1795, the British Navy's official grog ration (the highlight of the sailor's day) was a mixture of rum, lemon juice and water. Occasionally the juice from limes was substituted, which caused American sailors to taunt the British by calling them "limeys." (Lime juice in fact proved to be less effective against scurvy, because it was later found to contain less vitamin C.)

Of course, we still reach for lemons with honey for a cold; and some swear by a daily glass of lemon juice and water to promote longevity.

While some age-old folk remedies were a bit far fetched, most have a scientific basis. Today's scientists have confirmed that the vitamins C and E and beta carotene in lemon juice may help prevent cancer, restore elasticity to aging arteries and help bones retain calcium.

Lemon Lite-Muffins

Light on calories and tangy with lemon, this is "ultralite" baking at its best.

2 cups unbleached all-purpose flour
1¼ teaspoons baking soda
½ teaspoon salt
⅓ cup granulated sugar
Zest from 1 large lemon
2 large eggs
½ cup applesauce *(in place of ½ cup vegetable oil)*
½ cup lemon juice

Position rack in center of oven, preheat oven to 375 degrees F., and coat muffin wells with nonstick cooking spray.

In a 2½ quart mixing bowl sift flour, baking soda, salt, sugar and lemon zest. Stir to blend and make a well in center.

In a 1½ quart bowl whisk eggs thoroughly until light and frothy, then add applesauce and lemon juice. Beat well. Add applesauce mixture to flour mixture and stir until flour is just moistened. Batter should immediately appear foamy. Spoon quickly into prepared muffin wells.

Bake at 375 degrees F. for 20 minutes. Cool muffins in pan for 15 minutes before removing from wells to a wire rack.

Makes about 12 2½" muffins.

*Each muffin contains about: 117 calories, 3g protein, 24g carbohydrate, 1g fiber, **1g fat**, 35mg cholesterol, 186mg sodium.*

New Wrinkles on Prunes

Prune promoters have been struggling for years to project this humble fruit, but in spite of the millions spent on advertising, Americans have always looked askance at them or thought them a joke.

Not so in other countries: in France, for instance, prunes have always been highly regarded. The mainstay of the economy in the Lot Valley in southwest France is the renowned *pruneau d'Agen*—small, handsome, black or blue-black, and packed with intense fruit flavor overlaid with a nutty, smoky taste.

The prune originated in Western Asia then came to Eastern Europe with 13th century crusaders. Local legend relates that the *Agen* prune was first mentioned in Renaissance texts, considered a valuable export from the region by the 17th century, and the prime favorite for nearly two hundred years.

The French don't hesitate to eat prunes in innovative ways, but they prefer them either plain, dusted with sugar, stuffed with marzipan paste (ground almonds), soaked in Armagnac brandy, or used as the central ingredient in innumerable tarts and flans. The shops of southwest France and roadside stands along the Lot Valley offer delicious plum brandies and a prune-nut candy called *prunandises*.

It was in 1856 that Pierre Pellier brought cuttings of *La Petite d'Agen* prune plum from France to California, as the beginning of the California prune industry. The main prune variety today, descended from *La Petite d'Agen*, is the California French Prune.

Now a change is coming to America. Recent discoveries here have caused food chemists to take a fresh interest in the dried plum; purées of prunes and prune butter *(lekvar)* have been found to be natural fat substitutes for baking muffins and quick-breads, brownies, cookies and gingerbreads. With this fresh perspective, they are now considered a valuable ingredient in baking.

Who knows?—Americans may reverse the trend in *nouvelle cuisine*, and actually teach the French a new technique in the kitchen.

Prune Pecan Lite-Bread

Home-made prune purée takes only minutes to prepare (see page 180); otherwise use commercial ready-made prune butter as a handy convenience. Look for it in the jam and jelly section or baking section of the supermarket, or order by mail (see Appendix 3).

¾ cup prune purée or prune butter *(in place of ¾ cup shortening)*
¾ cup prune juice
2 teaspoons grated orange peel
1 cup toasted wheat germ
¾ cup whole-wheat flour
½ cup unbleached all-purpose flour
⅔ cup light brown sugar, firmly packed
1 teaspoon baking powder
½ teaspoon *each* baking soda and salt
Whites of 2 large eggs
½ cup chopped pecans

Position rack in center of oven, preheat oven to 350 degrees F., and coat a 9 x 5 x 3" loaf pan with nonstick cooking spray.

In saucepan mix prune purée or prune butter, juice and peel; bring just to boiling. Remove from heat; set aside.

In a 2½ quart mixing bowl combine wheat germ, flours, brown sugar, baking powder, baking soda and salt; stir to blend and make a well in center. Add remaining ingredients and mix completely. Spread batter in prepared pan.

Bake at 350 degrees F. for about 50 minutes, or until a toothpick inserted in center comes out clean. Cool in pan 10 minutes, then turn onto rack to cool completely.

Makes one 9 x 5 x 3" loaf, about 16 slices.

*Each slice contains about: 155 calories, 4.5g protein, 29g carbohydrate, 3g fiber, **3.5g fat**, 0 cholesterol, 124mg sodium.*

Pumpkin Spread

This spread goes perfectly with the muffins on the opposite page and the Pumpkin Currant Loaf on page 69, and is also delicious on toast or English muffins.

3 cups pumpkin purée (29 oz can)
1 (1¾ oz) package pectin powder
1 teaspoon *each* ground cinnamon and ground ginger
½ teaspoon *each* ground cloves and ground nutmeg
4½ cups granulated sugar

In a 2½ quart mixing bowl stir together pumpkin purée, pectin and spices until well blended. Turn into a large saucepan and stir over medium-high heat until boiling hard. Add sugar and bring to full rolling boil. Boil 1 minute, stirring constantly. Remove pan from heat. Spoon into hot sterilized jars and cover immediately with a thin layer of hot paraffin wax.

Makes seven 8-oz jars.

*One tablespoon contains about: 33 calories, 0 protein, 8.5g carbohydrate, **0 fat**, 0 cholesterol, .5mg sodium.*

Pumpkin Bran Lites

Pumpkin and orange make perfect go-togethers. Here they are in a healthy lowfat muffin that's just right for a good start to the day with a tall glass of fresh orange juice and a steaming mug of coffee.

1 cup oat bran
1 cup unbleached all-purpose flour
2 teaspoons baking powder
¼ teaspoon salt
1 tablespoon grated orange peel
⅔ cup light brown sugar, firmly packed
Whites of 2 large eggs
½ cup nonfat skim milk
1 cup canned pumpkin purée
2 tablespoons vegetable oil

Coat muffin wells with nonstick cooking spray.

In a 2½ quart mixing bowl sift bran, flour, baking powder and salt. Stir in orange peel and brown sugar to blend, and make a well in center.

In a 1½ quart bowl whisk egg whites until light and frothy. Add milk, pumpkin and oil. Beat well. Add to flour mixture and stir just until flour is moistened. Spoon into prepared muffin wells.

Bake in a preheated oven at 425 degrees F. for 20 minutes. Remove from pan and turn onto wire rack. Serve warm.

Makes about 12 2½" muffins.

*Each muffin contains about: 137 calories, 3.5g protein, 27g carbohydrate, 2g fiber, **3g fat**, 0 cholesterol, 119mg sodium.*

Cottage Cheese: A New Look at an Old Favorite

Cottage cheese has been around for literally ages, popular in many lands, and a mainstay of early American colonists who made it in their kitchens. We generally think of cottage cheese when our thoughts turn to dieting: eating it "as is," or as a scoop with light salads, or partnered with crunchy vegetables or sprinkled with fresh herbs and spices.

Now the familiar cheese is being given fresh appreciation with the knowledge that it can replace butter in many baking recipes, and give muffins a richness and wholesome flavor with fewer calories.

Cottage cheese is usually made with skim milk, a culture, and a cream dressing; however it pays to be a label reader as cottage cheese comes in many styles. Each is packed with healthy goodness, but the calorie-count and grams of fat can vary enormously, from 163 calories and 2.3 grams of fat in a cup of 1% fat cottage cheese to 239 calories and 9.5 grams of fat in a cup of 4% fat style.

Most markets stock creamed cottage cheese (4% fat) in small curd, which tends to be slightly firm, and large curd, which is generally more tender and velvety.

Lowfat cottage cheese will sometimes be labeled "Light," and contain either ½%, 1%, 1½% or 2% milkfat. Uncreamed or dry cottage cheese contains less than ½% milkfat and is a curd without added cream. Baker's cheese (sometimes referred to as Hoop cheese) has a finer texture and more moisture than creamed or dry cottage cheese. Nonfat cottage cheese contains less than ½% milkfat, and a dressing of nonfat milk solids.

Although the recipe on the opposite page uses nonfat cottage cheese, you may like to experiment with the different styles available in the dairy case to see the differences in baking results, in texture and flavor.

Walnut Spice Wunderbars

These crunchy golden bars have old-fashioned taste with a new-fashioned twist—the addition of cottage cheese.

1⅞ cups unbleached all-purpose flour
½ cup granulated sugar
1 teaspoon *each* baking powder and baking soda
½ teaspoon *each* ground allspice and ground cinnamon
¼ teaspoon salt
Whites of 3 large eggs
¾ cup nonfat skim milk
¾ cup nonfat cottage cheese
2 tablespoons vegetable oil
1 tablespoon lemon juice
Grated zest of 1 lemon
¼ cup finely chopped walnuts

Position rack in center of oven, preheat oven to 375 degrees F. and lightly coat a shallow 8" square pan with nonstick cooking spray.

In a 2½ quart mixing bowl sift flour, sugar, baking powder, baking soda, allspice, cinnamon and salt. Stir to blend and make a well in center.

In a 1½ quart bowl whisk egg whites until light and foamy. Add milk, cottage cheese, oil, lemon juice and zest. Beat thoroughly. Add all at once to flour mixture and stir just until flour is moistened. Gently fold in walnuts to distribute evenly. Spoon into prepared pan.

Bake at 375 degrees F. for about 45 minutes, or until a test toothpick inserted in center comes out clean. Cool 15 minutes and cut into bars while still in pan.

Makes 16 bars about 2" x 2".

Each bar contains about: 119 calories, 4g protein, 19g carbohydrate, .5g fiber, 3g fat, 1mg cholesterol, 150mg sodium.

Troubleshooting

You followed the recipe directions, but you still got strange results? Were your muffins too flat or too high, too dark or too pale, too dry or too soggy? Did your baking take too long or have awful shrinkage? Let's find out what went wrong, so you'll be prepared for the next try. Here are a few common problems and their probable causes:

What's your problem?	It could be due to one or more of these reasons
Baking slow?	❑ You hadn't preheated the oven. ❑ Your oven hadn't reached the right temperature. ❑ You set the temperature too low. ❑ You have aluminum foil in the bottom of the oven. ❑ You peeked too often and opened the oven door frequently. ❑ You had too many pans on the rack. ❑ You have an old oven out of calibration.
Muffins unevenly shaped?	❑ Batter was uneven in pans. ❑ Pans were touching one another or oven walls. ❑ You didn't mix the batter enough. ❑ The batter was too liquid. ❑ You peeked in during baking. ❑ Your range isnt level.
Muffins high in middle?	❑ You overmixed the batter. ❑ You used too much flour. ❑ The temperature was too high. ❑ Baking time was too long. ❑ Pans were touching one another or oven walls. ❑ You live at a high altitude, and need to reduce leavening.

Muffins flat, or fell dismally when you took them from the oven?	❑ Check the age of your baking powder (maybe you should throw out that old box). ❑ You put in too little baking powder. ❑ You added too much shortening or sugar. ❑ The batter was too thin, with too much liquid. ❑ You used eggs that were too cold or old. ❑ Your pans were too small. ❑ You peeked in too often during baking.
Muffins were unevenly brown, or too dark on the bottom?	❑ Your pans have darkened or dulled with age, or are made of glass. ❑ Your pans are warped and dented. ❑ Your oven hadn't reached the right temperature. ❑ Your rack was not positioned in the middle of the oven. ❑ Your oven was lined with aluminum foil. ❑ You peeked too often. ❑ You needed a tent of aluminum foil over large-size quick-breads for the last 15 minutes, to prevent over-browning.
Muffins shrink?	❑ Oven temperature was too high. ❑ Baking time was too long. ❑ You used too little leavening. ❑ The batter was overmixed.
Muffins dry?	❑ Oven temperature was too high. ❑ Baking time was too long. ❑ Flour was too dry due to improper storage. ❑ You needed more liquid or fat. ❑ You used old baking powder.

Muffin texture uneven?	❑ There was too much liquid. ❑ You didn't mix enough. ❑ Oven temperature was set too low. ❑ Baking time was too short.
Muffins have weird tunnels?	❑ You mixed too long. ❑ You used an electric mixer. ❑ You had too much baking powder. ❑ Oven temperature was too high.
Muffins not done, or soggy in the center?	❑ Oven temperature was too high. ❑ Muffin wells were overfilled. ❑ Addition such as fruit was too juicy. (You need to drain it well and toss it in some of the flour from recipe.) ❑ Frozen fruit was thawing inside muffins while baking.
Muffins cracked on top?	❑ Is that all you have to complain about? Then you're a pro! Even the experts' muffins have cracks!

Appendix 2

Conversion Charts

Volume:

U.S. Measure	U.S. (fluid ounces)	Imperial (fluid ounces)	Metric (milliliters)
1 teaspoon	¼	¼	5
1 tablespoon	½	½	15
2 tablespoons	1	1	30
¼ cup	2	2	60
⅓ cup	3	3	90
½ cup	4	4	120
⅔ cup	5	5	145
¾ cup	6	6	175
1 cup	8	8	235
1 pint	16	16½	475
1 quart	32	33	945
1 gallon	128	133	1.89 liters

U.S. fluid ounce   = 29.6 ml   Imperial fluid ounce   = 28.4 ml
U.S. standard cup = 8 fl oz   Imperial standard cup = 10 fl oz
            pint = 16 fl oz   pint = 20 fl oz

Weight:

U.S./Imperial (ounces)	Metric (grams)
½	14
1	28
2	57
3	85
4	113
5	142
6	170
7	198
8	227
12	340
16 (1 lb)	454

Oven Temperatures:

Fahrenheit	Centigrade	British Gas Mark	Heat Level
225	110	¼	very cool
250	130	½	very cool
275	140	1	cool or slow
300	150	2	cool or slow
325	170	3	warm
350	180	4	moderate
375	190	5	moderately hot
400	200	6	fairly hot
425	220	7	hot
450	230	8	very hot
475	240	9	very hot

Adjustment for high altitude: (for U.S. measures, see page 44)

Adjustment	1,000 meters	1,500 meters	2,000 meters
Baking powder: for each 5ml, cut by:	1.0ml	1.0 to 1.25ml	1.25ml
Sugar: for each 250ml, cut by:	15-30ml	30-60ml	45-60ml
Liquid: for each 250ml, add:	15-30ml	30-60ml	45-60ml

At high altitudes, you may sometimes need to reduce shortening by 15-30ml, since fat, like sugar, weakens cell structure.

Appendix 3

Shopping Guide

If you want to include unusual flours, grains, seeds and spices in your baking, look in your local telephone directory for addresses of health-food stores; and check the listings of kitchen-specialty shops for good selections of quality baking pans and other equipment. Otherwise, if you have difficulty in locating special supplies, the following addresses will be helpful.

Arkansas

Shiloh Farms
P.O.Box 97, Highway 59
Sulphur Springs, AR 72768
Telephone: 501-298-3297
Whole grains and flours. Send $1 (refundable) for catalog

California

Irish Imports
738 N. Vine Street
Hollywood, CA 90028
Telephone: 213-467-6714
Imported coarse-ground whole-wheat flours

Williams-Sonoma, Inc.
Mail Order Department
P.O. Box 7456
San Francisco, CA 94102-7456
Telephone: 800-541-2233
Quality kitchen equipment. Ask for catalog

Jordano's Kitchen Supply
614 Chapala Street
Santa Barbara, CA 93101
Telephone: 805-965-3031
Quality kitchen equipment and groceries

Maryland

The Store Ltd.
The Village of Cross Keys
5100 Falls Road
Baltimore, MD 21210
Telephone: 301-323-2350
Quality kitchen equipment

Massachusetts

Erewhon Trading Company
342 Newbury
Boston, MA 02115
Telephone: 617-262-3420
Assortment of grains, seeds and nuts. Ask for catalog

Mississippi

Eden Foods, Inc.
701 Tecumseh Road
Clinton, MS 49236
Telephone: 517-456-7424
Ask for nearest store retailing Eden products.

New York

Bridge Company
214 East 52nd Street
New York City, NY 10022
Telephone: 212-688-4220
Quality kitchen equipment. Ask for catalog

Dean & De Luca
Mail Order Department
560 Broadway
New York City, NY 10012
Telephone: 212-431-1691

Quality groceries and kitchen equipment. Ask for catalog

Hoffritz
515 West 24th Street
New York City, NY 10011
Telephone: 212-924-7300

Quality kitchen equipment. Ask for catalog

H. Roth & Son
1577 First Avenue
New York City, NY 10028
Telephone: 212-734-1111

Quality kitchen equipment, grains and spices. Ask for catalog

Birkett Mills
163 Main Street
Penn Yan, NY 14527
Telephone: 315-536-3311

Assortment of flours. Ask for price list

Pennsylvania

Flory Distributing Co.
South Broad Street
Lititz, PA 17543
Telephone: 717-626-2269

Assortment of flours, molasses, honey and seeds. Ask for price list

Walnut Acres Organic Farms
Box 8
Penns Creek, PA 17862
Telephone: 800-433-3998

Whole grains and flours. Ask for catalog

Stonehill Farm Foods Corp.
P.O. Box 158
Schwenksville, PA 19473
Telephone: 215-287-7655,
201-744-6413

Fruit butters and full-fruit spreads

Rhode Island

Gray's Mill
P.O. Box 422
Adamsville, RI 02801
Telephone: 508-636-2913

Freshly stone-ground flours

Tennessee

Falls Mill
134 Falls Mill Road
Belvidere, TN 37306
Telephone: 615-469-7161

Coarse-ground whole-wheat flours and wheat bran.

Texas

Arrowhead Mills
P.O. Box 2059
Hereford, TX 79045
Telephone: 806-364-0730

Assortment of grains, flours, nuts and cereals. Ask for nearest retailer

Wisconsin

The Spice House
P.O. Box 1633
Milwaukee, WI 53201
Telephone: 414-768-8799

Wide range of quality herbs and spices

Selected References

Beard, James. *Beard on Bread*. New York, New York: Alfred Knopf, Inc., 1973

Bredon, Juliet and Mitrophanow, Igor. *The Moon Year, a Record of Chinese Customs and Festivals*. New York, New York: Paragon Book Reprint Corp., 1966

Clayton, Bernard. *New Complete Book of Breads*. New York: Simon & Schuster, 1987

David, Elizabeth. *English Bread and Yeast Cookery*. New York: The Viking Press, 1977

Fiske, Rosalie Cheney and Potee, Joanne Koch. *The Bread Baker's Manual*. Englewood Cliffs, New Jersey: Prentice-Hall, Inc., 1978

Furnas, J.C. *The Americans*. New York, New York: G.P. Putnam's Sons, 1969

Hillman, Howard. *Kitchen Science*. Boston, Massachusetts: Houghton, Mifflin Company, 1989 (revised edition)

Ickis, Marguerite. *The Book of Festivals and Holidays The World Over*. New York, New York: Dodd, Mead & Company, 1970

Johnson, Ellen Foscue. *The Garden Way Bread Book*. Charlotte, Vermont: Garden Way Publishing, 1979

Jones, Judith and Evan. *The Book of Bread*. New York: Harper & Row, 1982

Krythe, Maymie R. *All About American Holidays*. New York, New York: Harper & Brothers, 1962

London, Mel. *Bread Winners Too*. Emmaus, Pennsylvania: Rodale Press, 1984

Morton, Julia. *Fruits of Warm Climates*. Miami, Florida: Creative Resources Systems, 1987

Myers, Robert J. *Celebrations: The Complete Book of American Holidays*. Garden City, New York: Doubleday & Company, Inc. 1972

Root, Waverley. *Food*. New York, New York: Simon & Schuster, 1980

Root, Waverley and de Rochemont, Richard. *Eating in America*. New York, New York: William Morrow and Company, Inc., 1976

Schneider, Elizabeth. *Uncommon Fruits and Vegetables*. New York, New York: Harper & Row, Publishers, 1986

Tannahill, Reay. *Food in History*. New York, New York: Stein and Day Publishers, 1973

Tuleja, Tad. *Curious Customs*. New York, New York: Harmony Books, 1987

Weaver, William Woys. *America Eats*. New York, New York: Harper & Row, 1989

Index

Index to Recipes